Praise for *Unear*

"We, as followers of Jesus, so often lose sight of the end of the story and get wrapped up only in the present. The Body of Christ needs to be reawakened to the unshakeable HOPE we have in Jesus. *Unearthing Heaven* is a needed wave of grace as Mike O'Quin shares how we can live today with both the fear of God and great hope as we imagine ourselves standing before Jesus and hearing him say, 'Well done, good and faithful servant!' With the hope of an expected future, we all can find strength to endure the challenges and sacrifices of today in the name of Jesus."

— **Jimmy Seibert**, author of *Passion and Purpose* and president of Antioch Ministries International

"The meaningful and regular consideration of one's personal evaluation by Jesus Christ is a life-changer. Other than my own personal salvation, this consideration has done more to impact my life than anything else. Mike O'Quin has done the body of Christ a huge favor in writing about the topic. Though I have considered the topic before and have read several volumes on the topic, this one moved me in many new ways to strive to please my king, Jesus. I am confident you'll be blessed, as I was, in reading this book."

— **Dr. Bill F. Korver**, president of Carolina College of Biblical Studies

"The Judgment Seat of Christ is one of the least talked-about and least understood teachings of scripture among the church today. Yet it is one of the most liberating doctrines in the

Bible and should profoundly impact how we conduct our lives. Mike does a fantastic job in *Unearthing Heaven* of making the biblical teaching of God's judgment of believers accessible and inspirational. Every Christ-follower needs to pick up this book and think deeply about its claims!"

— **Mick Murray**, author of *The Father's Heart* and co-host of the *Ideology* podcast

"In the midst of a time with significant cultural change, the call to live in light of eternity is perhaps one of the most important messages for the believer. Mike O'Quin challenges us to re-evaluate our motivations and discover anew the power of living from an eternal vision. He lives this message in his own life, and from this place of authority, he will challenge you to do the same."

— **Drew Steadman**, executive director of Antioch U.S. and author of *The Gospel According to Culture*

"When I was a little boy I noticed my mother sitting in the chair where she prayed every morning. She was crying. I said, 'Mommy, what's wrong?' She looked at me and smiled. 'Honey, I'm just imagining the moment when I will get to see the face of Jesus.' Perhaps no moment has ever touched me so deeply. I've heard it said that when Christians focus too much on the afterlife we become irrelevant in this life. In this powerful book, Mike O'Quin shatters that ridiculous notion, showing us that when we have the courage and faith to live passionately for the moment we will see Jesus in all of his glory, *everything* changes."

— **Paul Richardson**, international director of Mustard Seed International and author of *A Certain Risk*

"Have you ever wondered what exactly Paul means when he, inspired by the Spirit, exhorts us to: 'Set your heart on things above...' and then in the next verse: 'Set your mind on things above ...' (Colossians 3:1,2)? I mean, how do we apply this command practically? Mike O'Quin helps us understand this command, and more importantly, he inspires to want to live it out. *Unearthing Heaven* motivates us to live for THAT DAY when we stand before Christ and give account of our lives, making this reality understandable and motivational. Thanks, Mike, for inspiring us, sobering us, and refreshing us with a fresh look at a belief that's core to a Christian worldview."

— **Ron Parrish**, author of *From Duty To Delight* and *Strengthening Your Spiritual Core*

"Our imaginations are powerful. They are the driving force behind fear, anxiety, jealousy, vengeance, and a host of other evils. But Mike O'Quin argues that those same powerful imaginations, when fixed upon what is of eternal value—such as the smile of Jesus when we meet Him face to face—will give us a fresh purpose and joy in living. I've witnessed Mike's life—a life of purpose and joy that has touched the people of several nations. His life has been changed by this message, and yours will be too."

— **Jim Baton**, author of *A Way Out of Hell* and *Hope is a Dangerous Place*

"Engaging my holy imagination about things like heaven and (gasp!) heavenly rewards has changed how I work, serve, and live, and Mike's insights and clarity have brought fresh encouragement and hope during a difficult pandemic. I'm reminded that nothing I do, no matter how seemingly purposeless or meaningless, is unseen by my Savior and this humbling, hopeful truth gives me new vision for the road ahead."

— **Sarah Guerrero**, author of *Break Through* and *Let's Start With Love*

"Mike O'Quin makes me think and makes me laugh. This book on heaven's rewards inspires me towards a closer walk with Jesus and a healthier connecting between my faith and my works for Him."

— **Eric Bryant**, executive pastor of Gateway Church Austin and author of *Not Like Me*

Unearthing Heaven

Why Tomorrow's Reward Matters Today

7-8-21

Joe Ben and Sara,

we have so appreciated your encouragement over the years, are so honored by your very generous support- THANK YOU!

Mike O'Quin Jr.

I pray you would serve the bright smile of the king over your life as you serve in His kingdom.

Love and Thanks,

MANTAP
PUBLISHING

2 Cor. 13:14

www.UnearthingHeaven.com

Cover design by Hilary Brewer • hilarybrewer.com

Cover photo by Caio Freitas • cviophotos.com

Mantap Publishing • mantappublishing.com

Contact the author on his blog: mikeoquin.com

ISBN: 0578890607

ISBN-13: 978-0-578-89060-9

Library of Congress Control Number: 2021907758

To Naomi

Your tender heart towards the Lord
inspires your daddy deeply

My reward is with me,
and I will give to each person
according to what they have done.

– Jesus Christ, Revelation 22:12

CONTENTS

Introduction • Missing Treasure Chest   1

One • Brushing Away Heaven's Reward   9

Two • A House Tested   37

Three • A Raised Platform   53

Four • The Crown of Awkwardness   69

Five • The Crown of Glory   91

Six • The Crown of Life   101

Seven • The Crown of Righteousness   117

Eight • The Crown of Exultation   133

Nine • Struggle Meets Heaven   153

Ten • Rediscovering Heaven   167

Acknowledgments   199

About the Author   199

Other Books by Mike O'Quin Jr.   201

Recommended Resources For Further Study   205

Endnotes   207

INTRODUCTION

MISSING TREASURE CHEST

I'm standing in front of a room of about 60 people, preaching at an English-speaking international church service. This is a small fellowship of expatriates living in Indonesia, most of them missionaries serving cross-culturally or teachers at the international school where the church meets.

"How many of you have thought about your reward in heaven this week?"

No hands go up.

"How about this month?"

One hand gingerly lifts in the air.

"Okay, how about this year? How many of you have thought about your coming reward in heaven at some point this year?"

A few hands are now up, no more than five.

Most of these people are living overseas because they love Jesus and want to see His Kingdom advanced. They are risk-taking, Bible-loving believers, and yet only about 8% of them had thought at all about their reward in heaven in the last 365 days.

For the last few years as I've had opportunities to teach on the subject of heaven's rewards, I've taken the same informal poll. I would estimate that less than 10% of believers I've asked have given any thought to their reward in heaven in the previous year. Whether I'm in the U.S. or overseas, I find that the topic of heaven's honor is barely a blip on our theological screens.

How about you—how would you have answered that question? When was the last time your imagination was stirred by your reward in heaven?

The Unthought-Of Day

Jesus often taught on the promise of reward of heaven, and the prospect pulsated among His first followers. A cursory reading of the New Testament will have you bumping frequently into the theme of heaven's honor as a primary life motivation.

I imagine my poll's result would be much different if we went back to the first-century church and sat among a group of persecuted believers crammed into someone's simple home. "How many of you have thought about your reward in heaven today?" we'd ask them. I bet every hand would shoot up.

The early church fathers and reformers pondered it often. Sometimes they debated over it because the theology of coming rewards was so central for them and crucial in understanding the Kingdom of God.

Martin Luther reportedly said, "I have two days in my calendar, this day and that Day."[1] "That Day" referred to the moment of standing before Christ and receiving his master's accolade for the way he had lived his life on earth.

The first century and early church would be aghast at our apathy toward the honor of heaven. Even leaders from more recent church history would be shaking their heads in bewilderment.

Heroes in the faith like Hudson Taylor, Amy Carmichael and Nikolaus Von Zinzendorf (more on him later) had "that Day" planted vividly in their imaginations, and it deeply inspired them in their day-to-day lives. Charles Spurgeon, the renowned 19ᵗʰ-century English minister known as the "prince of preachers," said this coming Day of honor put a pep in his step for his long race: "There is a crown for me. Then will I gird up my loins and quicken my pace, since the crown is so sure to those who run with patience."[2]

Jim Elliot, a young man who was martyred in 1952 as he and four other missionaries were trying to reach the Huaorani people of Ecuador, famously wrote this in the margins of his journal four years earlier: "He is no fool who gives up what he cannot keep to gain what he cannot lose."[3]

Influential author and evangelical apologist C.S. Lewis marveled at our indifference to what he called "the unblushing promises of reward and the staggering nature of the rewards promised in the Gospels."[4] In his writings, Lewis cut against the common assumption that thinking about heaven too much makes us irrelevant on earth, an idea best summed up in the adage, "Don't be so heavenly minded that you become no earthly good." Lewis argues instead:

> It is since Christians have largely ceased to think of the other world that they have become so ineffective in this. Aim at heaven and you will get earth "thrown in": aim at earth and you will get neither.[5]

I'll unpack a little more from Lewis' writings on this subject later, because they are worth digging into, but for now I'm wondering: how did we go from richly imagining heaven's rewards to barely thinking about them at all in just a few short generations of Jesus-followers? Why are we so rarely stirred by the eternity-lighting smile waiting for us in heaven?

I can say from my own early spiritual formation that this impactful truth was nowhere to be found. From age 10 when I tearfully said yes to Jesus at a Christian summer camp altar call, through my teenage years when God drew me back to Himself after some junior high drifting, to getting involved and discipled in a lively youth group at a Bible-believing church during high school, I can't remember ever thinking about what waits for me on the other side of salvation.

When it was time to go to college, I chose a Christian school, figuring that kind of environment would help me keep growing spiritually. I moved from Mississippi to Texas to attend Baylor University, jumped into student ministries on campus and joined a vibrant local church.

It wasn't until that freshman year in college that I first encountered the life-transforming truth of what the Bible calls the "Judgment Seat of Christ." It was so impactful that I can even remember the room where I was sitting when I learned about it for the first time. Small room. Blue walls. A row of folding chairs lined up in front of a small television screen that was set on a rolling cart. The class met on Sunday mornings as a breakout session after the large group gathering of the college group, which was so large it had its own worship service. I chose a class with an intriguing title, something about living for eternity, which was led by Jamie Lash. He was a Bible teacher at Dallas Baptist University who would make the drive from Dallas to Waco every week to lead the small group at Highland Baptist Church.

Jamie gave an introduction to the class in front of the TV, popped a VHS cassette tape in the VCR, and played a video from

Rick Howard, a man with whom he would later write a book on this subject, entitled *This Was Your Life!*

In the first part of the video, Rick Howard vividly described a dream he had about the Judgment Seat of Christ, an experience that changed the course of his life. Throughout his gripping teaching and explanation of Bible passages on the theme, I could sense the presence of God; it was both beautiful and its sobering.

Jamie popped the VHS tape out of the player and there was holy, stunned silence. We were all gripped by an intense desire to live for God more wholeheartedly, some of us kneeling on the floor and crying out to God for His grace to do so. Up to that point, I had never known that my life would be evaluated in any way...I thought I had sidestepped all that when I came to Christ.

Jamie led us in prayer and taught us more over the next several weeks, each class building floor-by-floor on this life-changing truth. That truth rocked my world, and I'm praying that it will rock yours too in the pages to come.

Looking back, I wonder how I could have gone that long, from age 10 to 18, without once encountering this potent truth about the Judgment Seat of Christ. My spiritual formation and theology had been shaped in the southern United States, a bastion of evangelical Christianity known as the "Bible Belt," yet I can't recall any teaching or emphasis on rewards in heaven or God's evaluation of us there, a very strong theme in the Bible.

I thought a lot about getting saved, and what that meant for me and how I needed to share the Good News with others, but I hardly gave a thought about what waits on the other side of that salvation, namely heaven. If my brand of fervent, evangelical

Protestant Christianity were a restaurant, reward in heaven wouldn't even be on the menu.

Since first encountering this impactful truth as a late teen in that little breakout class, I'm sad to say that I have rarely heard it taught. And if my non-scientific and anecdotal polling is correct, most of us are not gripped by this coming day of heaven's honor—even people who are sent to the mission field as Christ's ambassadors.

What gives?

In this book I'd like to take you on a journey. First, I want to tackle that question, venturing three guesses why the teaching of that Day is so rare in our day. Let's get the objections out of the way right up front.

Then we will unpack the two metaphors the Apostle Paul used to help us understand the power of that Day, to give you some theological grounding for that hope. He actually presented the Judgment Seat of Christ in a way to stir longing in us and not dread.

Then we'll talk about our awkwardness over receiving honor from God and look at the four different crowns of the New Testament, each one championing a different Kingdom value. These crowns are meant to motivate you deeply (I realize crown-wearing doesn't do much for us these days…we'll work on that).

Next stop is to see how a vivid imagining of standing before Jesus at the Judgment Seat of Christ, with a big smile on His beaming face, can help us overcome addictive sins and common life struggles.

Finally, I'll argue that we have heaven all wrong, and that re-imagining it in a more biblical way will blow away the nonchalance in our minds and fire up our souls with longing.

Believe it or not, your latent desire for eternity is actually the truest thing about you, and tapping into it will make you feel like you've just discovered a hidden treasure chest of life motivation.

I hope you'll keep an open mind on this journey. We all get stuck for good reasons, our mindsets going back to familiar ruts again and again. I pray that my simple and conversational book will awaken a desire in you for that Day, so much so that you will consider living your life in light of a more vivid and rewarding eternity.

Mike O'Quin Jr.
Meadow Woods, Florida
May 2021

CHAPTER ONE

BRUSHING AWAY HEAVEN'S REWARD

If I told you that you were hard wired to be motivated by heaven's rewards, you would probably think to yourself...um...not so sure about that.

I'm guessing that deep down your soul agrees with me, but first we have to tackle some modern thinking around how we frame reward, what we assume about salvation and our culturally molded revulsion to judgment. After taking on these three objections, we will dive deeper into the theology of the Judgment Seat of Christ in the following chapters, so please hang with me if you are hung up on my central assertion, or at least long enough to give your soul a fighting chance to go on a treasure hunt.

1) Reward Seems Unspiritual

The first reason we neglect meditating on the staggering offer of our reward in heaven is that we have come to believe being rewarded for something makes it less pure, maybe even carnal.

For instance, if I were to go over to your house to mow your yard while you are on vacation, just to be nice, that would be a pure act of love. But if I go over to your house to mow your yard while you are on vacation, hoping and expecting that you will give me something in return, that would be manipulation. Let's say I brought it up when I needed your help, like, "Hey, I can't believe you're not going to help me out here. Remember last weekend when I mowed your grass while you were gone?" You would probably think, whoa...*what a manipulative guy*. Unless the two of us struck a deal first, my service to you would have to be a voluntary gift of my time, with no payment expected and definitely no strings attached.

That totally makes sense...on earth.

There's a fancy word that theologians sometime use called *anthropomorphism*, which means a description of God that comes from our experience as humans. When we read in the scriptures about God's arm, for instance, we get a sense of God working out something, as maybe our own arms would lift something. We might pray, "Stretch out Your arm, Lord," meaning, please God, perform a wonder in this matter.

Human language helps me understand a heavenly God. Through words and concepts I already understand, a little bit of understanding illuminates His character. But there is a limitation to anthropomorphisms, as J.I. Packer explains in his theological masterpiece *Knowing God*:

> Since we are more like God than is any other being known to us, it is more illuminating and less misleading for God to picture himself to us in human terms than any other...When faced with God's anthropomorphisms, however, it's easy to get hold of the wrong end of the stick. We have to remember that man is not the measure of His maker, and that when the language of human personal life is used of God, none of the

limitations of human creaturehood are thereby being implied—limited knowledge or power, or foresight, or strength, or consistency or anything of that kind.[6]

So, when we pray "O God, stretch out Your arm," that helps us picture God moving in a particularly difficult situation, but not necessarily that God has an elbow. The thought that altruism is pure and payback is impure makes sense on earth, but when we extrapolate it heavenward toward our relationship with God, it doesn't quite work. It's making God have an elbow.

With my friends, I may feel that any motivation to be rewarded for how I have served them makes the act itself impure, something more transactional than relational. Agreed. I then bring that assumption into my relationship with God, believing that no reward is needed from my service to Him because I want to show Him pure, altruistic love. However, in this subtle shift we have, to use Packer's analogy, grabbed the wrong end of the anthropological stick. The altruism-is-pure and expecting-reward-is-manipulation premise is based on an equal relationship (e.g., one friend mowing the grass for another equal friend).

But we aren't serving an equal, we are living for the Creator of the universe who is above us in every category and who stands at the end of time. Because He is so superior to us in every way and in every realm, our only proper orientation back to Him is one of subservience. That means our service to Him isn't an I'll-scratch-your-back, you-scratch-mine transaction, but rather that of an inferior serving a superior. We are the servants and He is the King. Now it's true that Jesus lifted our identity beyond that (in John 15:5 He called us friends), but in terms of who is serving whom, He is the ultimate Whom.

It may seem spiritual to say, "My only reward is serving You, Lord," but the writers of the New Testament would stare at us, cock their heads and say, "Huh?" Their cultural understanding was wrapped around the ways kings acted in governance and not based around our more egalitarian ideals. We Westerners don't understand royalty, but they got it. Servants served kings. Those kings would evaluate the service of their servants, and the ones who served well were affirmed and rewarded. The ones who served poorly were deemed foolish and stripped of privileges. A truth like this from Proverbs would have resonated with them:

When a king's face brightens, it means life;
his favor is like a rain cloud in spring.
(Proverbs 16:15)

First-century believers stayed motivated by the desire to brighten the face of their King Jesus with their life's service. Receiving honor from Him wasn't beneath them because His pleasure was their greatest hope.

Our Western culture has moved so far past an understanding of king-servant dynamics that when we read those parables in the New Testament, we understand them sideways. Our modern house of thought, when it comes to rewards, slid off that cultural foundation long ago.

The 18th-century German philosopher Immanuel Kant, in his "categorial imperative," insisted that service motivated by anything other than sheer duty defiles its purity. "Apart from moral conduct," he wrote, "all that man thinks himself able to do in order to become acceptable to God is mere superstition and religious folly." Yep, that makes more sense to the Western mind...get those impure thoughts out of your mind.

But back to the world of the New Testament. The apostles' teachings and a lot of Jesus' parables are based on the relationship between master and servant more than employer and employee. These word pictures are not about equals who are owed their reward, but rather about servants who are delighted that their master is pleased with them. Any reward from that superior authority is a deep honor. With this backdrop, Romanian pastor Josef Tson explains how to frame reward:

> Slaves can never claim wages or rewards. After they have done everything their master has commanded, they can only say: "We are unworthy slaves; we have only done our duty" (Luke 17:10). The master is in no way obligated by the work done by his slaves. However, he is free to "reward" his slaves, and whatever he gives them comes truly as a "reward" and not "wages." It comes from his generosity, not from his obligation.[7]

No question that slavery is evil and loathsome to us, as it should be. Yet that ugly reality of the first century was the cultural backdrop in which these parables were painted. The big take-away of these stories is that the Master is generous. What an honor to receive any sign of appreciation from Him at all! So no, we are not owed rewards, but wow, we receive them with gratitude because our generous Master delights to honor us.

Another thing that muddies the water for us is the word "reward" itself. It can be noble, or it can be self-serving, and we have mixed the two in our minds and therefore have deemed the whole concept carnal.

In his leadership book *The Motive,* Patrick Lencioni writes about two different motivations for those in authority, one focused on the perks and status of being a leader and one focused on serving the people of the organization.[8] The first motivation he calls Reward Oriented. This is like the CEO of an organization getting stoked about getting the top corner office and flying around to meetings in a company jet, and going on and on about it. The second he calls Responsibility Oriented. This is a purer motivation, one in which the leader's orientation is toward serving and caring for the people under him on the org chart. Sure, he may enjoy the perks of the C-suite, but the thing that gets him going in the mornings is serving people well and moving the organization's vision forward. We can understand that difference, as we have all known leaders who seem to point all the attention back to themselves. Those people focused on rewards are selfish, we can see clearly, while those focused on responsibility are selfless.

This is another principle, while being 100% true on earth, doesn't extrapolate well to heaven. Let's go back to Lewis' brilliant essay *The Weight of Glory* for a moment to help us understand this discrepancy. Here's how he delineates between the two kinds of rewards:

> We must not be troubled by unbelievers when they say that this promise of reward makes the Christian life a mercenary affair. There are different kinds of rewards. There is the reward which has no natural connection with the things you do to earn it and is quite foreign to the desires that ought to accompany those things. Money is not the natural reward of love; that is why we call a man mercenary if he marries a woman for the

sake of her money. But marriage is the proper reward for a real lover, and he is not mercenary for desiring it. A general who fights well in order to get a peerage is mercenary; a general who fights for victory is not, victory being the proper reward of battle as marriage is the proper reward of love. The proper rewards are not simply tacked on to the activity for which they are given, but are the activity itself in consummation.[9]

You are not an uncaring mercenary trying to get something "out of" God as if you were only serving Him for a big payday someday. You are a "real lover" in Lewis' words, one whose primary motivation is to win the heart of the beloved.

Marriage is the "proper reward" and consummation of a noble love pursuit. I worked hard during dating and courtship to win the heart of my beloved, who said yes to my marriage proposal and then became my wife. As I was pursuing her, writing sweet notes and planning creative dates, the thought never occurred to me, *Hey, wait a minute...am I being selfish here? Am I doing all this just to use Stephanie for my own self-interests? Shouldn't I be doing all this romantic stuff and expect nothing in return?* No way. I was pursuing her romantically because I wanted to win her heart and be with her forever, which was the reward of all that pursuit.

So as we think about reward, remember that we are not doing a friend a favor but rather serving a superior, and that there is a difference between a mercenary's payday and the reward of winning a beloved's heart. And if all that is not enough to flush this "no reward needed" belief out of our souls, remember that God has wired you for reward!

People diet because they hope to lose weight. Hard-working employees pull long hours because they hope they will get that promotion and raise. Performers rehearse hard for upcoming performances and athletes train hard for upcoming competitions. I wouldn't be writing this book in my free time right now if there wasn't some small hope of getting it published. There is always some inner motivation urging us on in any endeavor. We work hard because there is a reward at the end— a healthier body, a promotion, a trophy, recognition, bragging rights, etc.

I've heard this analogy before by Jamie Lash, the Bible teacher who opened my eyes to this life-changing concept. He asked what would happen on the first day of a college class if the professor said, "Hey, I just want everyone to know that you all get an A. It doesn't matter if you come to class or not, do the assignments, or take any of the tests. Everyone is guaranteed an A!"

What would that do to the morale of the class? After the initial euphoria subsided, how many students would keep showing up for lectures, doing their assignments and taking the tests? Very few, of course. Some brave ones might even exit the classroom as soon as the surprising announcement was made. We are motivated by reward, pure and simple.

When we lived in Indonesia, there was a popular television show I enjoyed watching called *Minta Tolong,* which basically means, "I need help!"[10] Every week a hidden camera crew sent out a down-trodden person into the streets to ask for help from strangers. I remember an episode in which an actress playing a destitute beggar went from person to person, asking for a blanket for her child. She was holding a ratty newspaper and offered to trade it if they would give her a blanket. Person after person said no. She would plead with them, "Please, my child is cold and doesn't have a blanket. Don't you have an extra one at your house?" They would brush her off and she would then go on to the next person. After numerous rejections, one kind soul finally said yes, giving the beggar lady a *selandang* sling she was using for her own child. The beggar then gave her newspaper to the kind lady, and inside it was a very large sum of money. The crew came out and interviewed the kind-hearted soul, who was overcome with emotion and didn't want to accept the money at first. She finally did at the interviewer's insistence as tears streamed down her shocked face.

How many of the people who said no would have said yes if they had known that inside that dirty newspaper was a hidden bundle of cash? Every single one of them, of course! They would have gladly done a good deed if they knew they were going to be rewarded for it. That's just the way we humans are wired. Knowing reward is coming and being motivated by it doesn't make your motivation dirty...it makes you human.

In the Sermon on the Mount, Jesus didn't say that seeking reward is wrong. Instead, His challenge was to consider which audience orientation we have in mind as we do good works, man's approval or God's affirmation. Whether our service be in the secret disciplines of giving, fasting or prayer, He urged us to live our lives for an audience of One: "Then your Father, who sees what is done in secret will reward you" (Matthew 6:4).

Heavenly treasure is eternal and man's approval is fickle. The exclamation point to this section of the Sermon on the Mount delineates between these two types of treasure and points us to the vastly superior one:

Do not store up for yourselves treasures on earth, where moths and vermin destroy, and where thieves break in and steal. But store up for yourselves treasures in heaven, where moths and vermin do not destroy, and where thieves do not break in and steal. For where your treasure is, there your heart will be also. (Matthew 6:19-21)

The point is to let your heart go after the better treasure, not to try to stamp out the motivation for reward in your heart.

Becoming nothing isn't Christianity. That's Buddhism. You were destined to be glorified (in a godly, God-honoring way), and you're going to have to get over it. You certainly can't get away from it. You are motivated by reward and wired for glory. Deep down you want to be honored for your achievements and that desire is not going away anytime soon. God knows this, because He created you this way, and so He offers you mind-blowing promises of moth-proof, rust-proof, thief-proof eternal reward. Brushing it off with "Nah, Lord. No recognition needed," is not being totally authentic with your honor-craving heart. You yearn to be esteemed and you can't spiritualize that away, despite how spiritual that may seem.

C.S. Lewis, in a famous quote, affirms the glory of reward and laments how easily we settle for lesser glories:

If we consider the unblushing promises of reward and the staggering nature of the rewards promised in the Gospels, it would seem that Our Lord finds our desires not too strong, but too weak. We are half-hearted creatures, fooling about with drink and sex and ambition when infinite joy is offered us, like an ignorant child who wants to go on making mud pies in a slum because he cannot imagine what is meant by the offer of a holiday at the sea. We are far too easily pleased.[11]

Somehow we have been tricked down here in the slums, pleased as punch with mud pies. If we were ever to stop playing with them for a minute, and imagine that holiday at the sea, our next thought would probably be...*that's wrong. Stop thinking about something so selfish.*

Paul the apostle, who lived very selflessly for the sake of the Gospel, did not consider being rewarded for proclaiming it selfish in the slightest. In the first few chapters of his letter to the Corinthians, he affirms his rights as an apostle (to have their respect, to eat food that had been sacrificed to idols, to receive financial support for his ministry), but then says he is willing to surrender all those God-given rights. Why? So that people wouldn't be offended by these issues and his message discredited. His eye was on a bigger prize:

I have become all things to all people so that by all possible means I might save some. I do all this for the sake of the gospel, that I may share in its blessings. (1 Corinthians 9:22b-23)

What were those "blessings"? He uses an analogy of an athlete in the very next verses to paint a picture of this glory pursuit:

Do you not know that in a race all the runners run, but only one gets the prize? Run in such a way as to get the prize. Everyone who competes in the games goes into strict training. They do it to get a crown that will not last, but we do it to get a crown that will last forever. (1 Corinthians 9:24-25)

His fear wasn't of selfish motives but rather being "disqualified for the prize" (verse 27), meaning missing out on receiving a lasting crown in heaven.

He ran after it hard and we can too, guilt free. So let's ask God, who finds our desires way too weak and our souls far too easily pleased, to stretch out our imaginations toward that Great Day and the staggering promise of Him rewarding us in heaven.

2) Salvation Seems to Negate Evaluation

The second reason I believe we ignore heavenly reward as our life motivation is a misunderstanding of salvation by grace. We marvel at the amazing truth of God's unmerited favor (which we should and which we will throughout all of eternity), but we fail to give much thought of what lies beyond that entryway.

It's fitting for believers to revel in the precious truth that we are saved one hundred percent by God's amazing grace. The entire movement of the Reformation is built on that one simple truth, *Sola Gratia*, by grace alone. In 1513, a young Catholic monk named Martin Luther encountered the truth of Romans 1:17: "For in the gospel the righteousness of God is revealed—a righteousness that is by faith from first to last, just as it is written: 'The righteous will live by faith.'" This revelation lit his striving heart and would eventually reengineer the entire church landscape. Later he wrote:

> This one and firm rock, which we call the doctrine of justification, is the chief article of the whole Christian doctrine, which comprehends the understanding of all godliness.[12]

Luther was right. The doctrine of justification *is* the "chief article" of Christian doctrine, the solid bedrock on which our faith stands. Righteousness is a free gift from God, totally dependent on Christ's sacrifice on the Cross. For those who call on Jesus (Romans 10:13), His blood covers all of their sins.

That's awesome! That's amazing! A free get-out-of-jail-free card! I deserve hell but I get heaven—that's really good news! The word Gospel actually means "good news," and it is. Wow, just wow.

But many of us stop right there, at the foundational doctrine of salvation, thinking that amazing grace is the end game in Christianity. We're riding on the train bound for glory with a free ticket in hand, and we kind of think it doesn't really matter how we live our lives. That golden ticket ensures our entrance through the pearly gates because we are saved by grace. Why worry about anything else? Nary a thought is given to "to work out your salvation with fear and trembling" (Philippians 2:12).

God's unmerited acceptance does not equal unmerited approval toward however which way we live our lives. I like how theologian D.M. Panton puts it: "God always gives undeserved salvation, He never gives undeserved praise."[13] Undeserved grace really is amazing, but that same salvation doesn't mean there is no evaluation. We have escaped God's wrath and judgment—*YES*—but that doesn't mean He is not going to judge, or evaluate us, as believers.

3) Evaluation Seems Harsh

You and I have a blind spot as we read the scriptures. The harder truths we tend to avoid, and this is one of them. We like to think of God as a loving deity who is in our corner to bless us as we go about our lives. That's totally true and worth celebrating. But thinking about God as over us, as a judge who has opinions of how we go about our lives...that truth tends not to get a lot of pulpit spotlight nor sell a lot of books.

Dr. Bill Korver, president of Carolina College of Biblical Studies, wrote his doctoral dissertation on heaven's rewards as motivation for Christian service and how most believers are fuzzy on the point about God having any intention of ever evaluating us. His research has been helpful to me in framing these arguments. In his dissertation (worth googling and reading), he shows how our common lack of understanding about heaven, due to the scarcity of teaching on the Judgment Seat of Christ, makes us passively okay with carnality. We retreat, both in the pew and in the pulpit, from these harder truths of the scriptures:

> It was true in the first century and it is true in the twenty-first century, there is a tendency for those who listen to God's messengers to react poorly to truth that is not pleasant. It is also a tendency for the messenger to not practice what he/she proclaims. To say one thing but do another. If the messenger does not resort to

hypocrisy such as this, there is another danger, that of altering the message from God, thus softening it to make it not so difficult for the hearer to bear.[14]

Judgment seems harsh, so we soften it. I soften it. Notice how I didn't even have the courage to use the J-word in subtitling this section. I wanted to make it easier to bear, so I'm writing about "evaluation" instead of...gulp...judgment. I chose a blander, more managerial word, just a spoonful of nicety to help the theological medicine go down.

Paul the apostle had no such cowardly qualms. In admonishing the Roman believers not to be judgmental toward each other on "disputable matters," he reminded them that they too would be judged by God one day:

> You, then, why do you judge your brother or sister? Or why do you treat them with contempt? For we will all stand before God's judgment seat. It is written: "'As surely as I live,' says the Lord, 'every knee will bow before me; every tongue will acknowledge God.'" So then, each of us will give an account of ourselves to God. (Romans 14:10-12)

Elsewhere, he challenged the believers in Corinth to orient their lives beyond the temporal and towards the eternal:

> We are confident, I say, and would prefer to be away from the body and at home with the Lord. So we make it our goal to please him, whether we are at home in the body or away from it. For we must all appear before the

judgment seat of Christ, so that each of us may receive what is due us for the things done while in the body, whether good or bad. (2 Corinthians 5:8-10)

In both of these passages, he is writing not to unbelievers but to believers. Paul reveled in the truth that we are one hundred percent saved by grace, but he also plainly taught that followers of Jesus would experience a thorough judgment. We moderns often focus solely on elementary truths and tend to sidestep these more sobering ones.

One thing that Paul's listeners had over us, to help them swallow these harder truths, is that their culture did not eschew any talk of judgment. Our culture has an emotive, knee-jerk reaction against even the concept of judgment. "Who are you to judge me?" we might hear someone say with a scowl, or "Why are you being so judgmental?"

In 2005, sociologists Christian Smith and Melinda Denton coined the term "moralistic therapeutic deism" to describe a common belief system of young people in the United States. In their book, *Soul Searching: The Religious and Spiritual Lives of American Teenagers,* they extensively researched young peoples' beliefs and boiled down the tenets of this moralistic therapeutic deism:

1. A God exists who created and ordered the world and watches over human life on earth.
2. God wants people to be good, nice, and fair to each other, as taught in the Bible and by most world religions.

3. The central goal of life is to be happy and to feel good about oneself.
4. God does not need to be particularly involved in one's life except when God is needed to resolve a problem.
5. Good people go to heaven when they die.[15]

See any judgment in there in any way, shape, form or creed? Not one whiff.

Moralistic therapeutic deism wasn't the worldview of the biblical writers. As theologian N.T. Wright explains:

The word judgment carries negative overtones for a good many people in our liberal and postliberal world. We need to remind ourselves that throughout the Bible, not least in the Psalms, God's coming judgment is a good thing, something to be celebrated, longed for, yearned over. It causes people to shout for joy and the trees of the field to clap their hands.[16]

"Judgment" might be a nasty word for us, but that may be because we have been basting in a consumeristic Christianity unknown to the early church. I have to remind myself that my perfect and impartial Creator has every God-given-to-Himself right to evaluate me. There is no higher authority in any realm—heaven or earth—who is more justifiable in judging me.

Evaluation? Judgment? I realize those words don't blend well with the warm and fuzzy feelings we normally associate with heaven. Thinking of a thorough assessment of our lives doesn't quite give us the feel-good vibes.

Let me assure you that heaven is going to be even warmer and fuzzier than you could ever imagine. It's going to be so glorious and resplendent with God's presence that you're going to get a new resurrection body just to be able to handle its intense pleasure. You will immensely enjoy unbroken fellowship with God in a beautiful place where His reign of love and grace go unchallenged by disappointment, disease and sin.

But that doesn't mean it won't initially also be intensely sobering. This evaluation of believers will take place at an event Paul called "the judgment seat of Christ." This is the place where you, as a blood-bought and grace-bestowed believer, will be eyeball to eyeball with Jesus Christ and He will evaluate how you lived your years on earth.

This fixed point in eternal time, which I imagine happening as an opening step in our new existence, is going to be intense. Your entire life will be evaluated by the Faultless One in the most penetrating light ever imagined. Every good work you did weighed against every motive. Every action you took and every word you spoke laid bare before Him in bright, white light. The writer of Hebrews, whose audience was a believing community, wrote about God's gaze this way: "Everything is uncovered and laid before the eyes of him to whom we must give account" (Hebrews 4:13). Yikes and yowza.

Lucky for us, this judgment (there, I said it) has to do with reward and not punishment. On that Day He is looking with His penetrating gaze for what He can reward. But that moment, the one in which we must give account of how we responded to His precious gift of salvation and how His grace worked through our lives, has to be slightly terrifying. There will be no excuses or half-baked justifications to hide behind. All things laid bare in the holy gaze of Him to whom we must give account.

Sounds a bit scary to me, and modern believers don't like scary. We'd rather imagine heaven as a place where Jesus is at the center but without any fire in His eyes. All hugs and smiles and no accountability. *Sweet By and By* without any soberness. While heaven is primarily a place of joy, it would be good to salt our lives with the knowledge that heaven is also a place of evaluation.

Think of a dentist appointment, one in which leading up to it you have been on top of your dental care game, brushing and flossing regularly. Even though you have been careful with your teeth, you are going to feel some uneasiness as your dentist shines a light in your mouth and pokes around with his pokey instruments to get a more thorough look. As your dental visit gets closer, you might imagine that feeling and do an extra good job the week before brushing and flossing, fearing that evaluation (we always tell our kids that if they haven't been flossing for six months, it's probably too late the morning of your appointment to start and make up for lost time). In most of our modern-day Christian teaching diet, we have been taught there is no dental visit coming. Your teeth have been pre-approved as clean and the dentist is not even going to take a peek inside your mouth! You get a lollipop at the end of the visit—no matter what!

But the Bible doesn't teach that. An examination is coming, a very thorough one. Salvation doesn't mean no evaluation. Even in this place where we get in 100% free by God's grace, there will be a soberness as we stand before Jesus at the Judgment of Christ and He shines His light on our lives.

A Sunday school teacher once told me as I was just stepping into the faith, "Jesus is your friend but not your buddy." Wise words. If we treat Jesus as one of the guys, just another roomie to trade head noogies with, we lose the respect that requires obedience. Yet if we see Him only as a stern schoolmaster over the solar system, taking names and dishing out demerits, we lose the friendship and intimacy He desires with us. The whole goal of the Cross is intimacy with God—as I said earlier Jesus calls us friends now. That is amazing and totally true, but brings with it some tension in our relationship with Him, just as there are multifaceted attributes in His very nature. Yes, He is good all the time, but that goodness is more fierce than buddy-buddy.

C.S. Lewis put this tension in story form in his first released book of the Narnia series, *The Lion, the Witch, and the Wardrobe*. I love this classic scene when the four children who stumbled into Narnia first hear about Aslan, the Christ character in Narnia, from Mr. and Mrs. Beaver:

"Is—is he a man?" asked Lucy.

"Aslan a man!" said Mr. Beaver sternly. "Certainly not. I tell you he is the King of the wood and the son of the great Emperor-Beyond-the-Sea. Don't you know who is the King of Beasts? Aslan is a lion—*the* Lion, the great Lion."

"Ooh!" said Susan, "I'd thought he was a man. Is he— quite safe? I shall feel rather nervous about meeting a lion."

"That you will, dearie, and no mistake," said Mrs. Beaver. "If there's anyone who can appear before Aslan without their knees knocking, they're either braver than most or else just silly."

"Then he isn't safe?" said Lucy.

"Safe?" said Mr. Beaver; "don't you hear what Mrs. Beaver tells you? Who said anything about safe? 'Course he isn't safe. But he's good. He's the King, I tell you."[17]

I'm so glad our King is good all the time, but I can't stretch that out to make Him harmless and "safe."

Sure, we're not supposed to be terrified of God, but I think we would do well with a tad more reverential fear. I think most of us sit on the "Jesus as buddy" end of the couch. He is that lovely man with feathered bangs who wouldn't hurt a fly, sort of like a sappy, sweet boyfriend.

There is a sweet intimacy in connecting with Jesus in an emotional, tender way...I do every single day. Did so this morning. Yet to grasp the fullness of who Jesus is, both as gentle Shepherd and fierce King, we would do well to meditate on the Judgment Seat of Christ.

When I think about that Day, it sobers me up and it should you, too. Jesus has fire in His eyes, not fairy sparkle dust. That fire pierces through every other façade and justification and sees deeply into our souls. Again, He is looking for that which can be rewarded, thankfully, but each one of us will have to go through that fire first to be counted worthy of His honor.

In order for this life-changing truth to do its work, we need to meditate not only on Jesus' tender love, but also His penetrating gaze. In His authority and perfection, He has the absolute right to evaluate our lives.

Our spiritual formation has been shaped by a me-first culture our entire lives, carefully protecting us from any theology that doesn't put us in the dead center of Christianity. *Yeah, but what's in it for me?* is the question we bring into any teaching, including this one. I understand that this sobering truth might not sit well with our entitlement-craving souls at first, but I want to encourage you to be open to its fierce beauty in the pages to come. Meditating on this hidden truth, and even imagining what it could look like for you, can transform your life just as it has done for believers in past centuries.

Hang on to these anchor points as we forge ahead: Reward isn't unspiritual. Grace-soaked, blood-bought believers are going to be judged. That final judgment over our lives may seem harsh, but that's because our culture, both inside and outside of the church, has been molding us to believe that we are above any evaluation. With these three fixed points in mind, we can now move back to God's heart, the *why* behind the Judgment Seat of Christ.

The Joy of a Proud Father

When my sister and I got good grades in school, which was always the case for her and sometimes the case for me, on report card day we got rewarded by a family night out at our favorite restaurant, Pizza Inn. We were allowed to order any kind of pizza and eat as much of it as we wanted, as well as drink all the soda we could down (a whole pitcher!). We each got a large handful of quarters to play music on the juke box (probably something from Journey or Queen) and to feed the arcade games Galaga or table-top Mrs. Pac Man to our video game-loving hearts' content. Ahh, the glory of the '80s.

But the best part of the whole evening was the smile on my dad's face. This lavish celebration was the backdrop, but what made the evening so special was that my dad was proud of us. He was in a good mood. There was a big smile on his face. We laughed a lot. His pleasure was even more enjoyable than the biggest pizza, the tallest pitcher of Coke and the highest score on Galaga. All those things were signs of his deep pride in us. "You guys worked hard this semester," he would say, "and your mom and I are so proud of you."

I can still remember the glow of that feeling, all these decades later. I can remember at the end of the semester opening up the brown envelope that held my grades, taking a peek and thinking, "All A's and B's...yes! Pizza Inn tonight!"

But even more than the Pizza Inn event, the thing that made it so special was that *my dad was proud of me.*

Now would I have worked hard for good grades during the semester even if there were no Pizza Inn celebration at the end? Probably so. But getting rewarded for working hard and knowing my dad would be proud of me in a celebratory environment gave me a little turbo boost during the year as I learned the material, did my assignments and took the tests. There was that sense that I was working toward something—a reward at Pizza Inn and a smile on my dad's face. It made the grinding through the spelling lists, memorizing times tables and finishing up homework at night so much more worth it.

We need to imagine our Father's face more as we are memorizing the times tables of life. On report card day, that smile on our Father's face will make all of the grind so worth it. God is proud of you in the here and now, and He is awaiting the Day when He can fully show you just how much.

God is looking forward to rewarding you in heaven. He's going to have a big smile on His face and a twinkle of joy in His eyes as you meet Him face-to-face for the very first time. He finally gets to announce, in front of all the heavenly hosts, "Well done!" His pride and pleasure are going to light up heaven. He has been waiting your entire life to honor you for the life you have lived.

We get a glimpse of the proud twinkle in our Father's eye in Jesus' Parable of the Talents. In this story it's very easy to only focus on who gets into the Kingdom of heaven and who doesn't. That's the most dramatic part of the story, but I want to pull one phrase out that you may have overlooked. This is what the master said to each of the two servants who had increased his investment:

> His master said to him, "Well done, good and faithful servant. You have been faithful over a little; I will set you over much. Enter into the joy of your master." (Matthew 25:21, 23, ESV)

Enter into the joy of your master. Our generous Master has a lot of joy and He wants to share it. God is in a good mood in heaven. We will enter that joy for all of eternity, and we can even taste of it now in this life. We can walk in an awareness that Jesus not only loves us, He *likes* us. He's even proud of us. He probably likes to pull pictures of us out of His big ol' wallet and show them to all the angels.

Wait a minute, I just said there is fire in Jesus' eyes as He evaluates our lives at His judgment seat, that place where no hidden thing or secret motive can hide in unblinking light, and now I'm saying that there is a glint of joy in His eyes as He has been waiting for this Day, longing to show you how proud He is of you.

So which is it?

Is he an objective judge or a proud father?

He's both.

One and the same. Fair and Gracious.

And that is the tension we will need to keep in mind to fully grasp the Judgment Seat of Christ, letting its full-orbed eventuality renew our thinking and transform our lives.

The point of the Judgment Seat of Christ is that after reviewing our lives in the intense light of His gaze, God can find the worthwhile and honor us for it. He wants to show you how proud He is of you.

Think of a proud coach on awards banquet night. He has been watching you all season, through grueling practices when you thought no one was watching, during games when you tried your best to perform under pressure, and behind the scenes in how you treated your teammates. Now it's time to honor you for how you carried yourself on and off the field.

He may put his players through tough practices and challenging games, but on this night he's in a very good mood. He has thought long and hard about every player and what award they deserve...Most Improved, Hardest Working, Best Attitude, etc. He is standing on that dais with his players in mind, beaming with pride and so looking forward to calling each one's name. Punishment is the last thing on his mind. This is all about public honor.

If you worked hard, you might be sitting in that audience at the awards banquet with a hope of winning an award. If you slacked off, you're still glad to see your teammates get awarded at the event, but you yourself wouldn't expect any public adulation.

And now the coach rises on the dais and begins to give out his well-thought-through awards. There is a smile on his face because he has been looking forward to this special evening. His opening speech is full of words of pride and honor. He is not looking to rehash mistakes made by his players during the season in front of their friends and family; he is looking to award that which is honorable.

I believe Jesus is greatly looking forward to this Day, a special awards banquet where He can finally let all of heaven know what He thinks of you. This occasion is all about bestowing honor, not dishing out correction.

Every time you gave selflessly, every time you made an unpopular stand for righteousness, every time you carved out time to seek Him in the secret place, every little Gospel seed you sowed, and every time compelled by His great love you showed love. You are overwhelmed that He saw every small decision to say yes to Him. There are hundreds of thousands of instances, each one recounted and affirmed. That little ministry deal you did so that those kids would be impacted? That was a big deal to Him and He wants all of heaven to know.

You can hardly believe it, but you know that every word that comes out the mouth of this Matchless One is true and pure, like gold refined in the fire. You dare not deflect His honor and He continues. On earth this would take forever, but in this realm you have forever, plus your memory has been fully restored, so you can now remember each one clearly as He brings them up one by one.

All these simple acts from your simple life, heralded in heaven by the King of Kings. It's almost too much to bear, and you are grateful His grace is sustaining you to be able to handle the honor, that His strength is enabling you to even stand before Him.

Now He is peering deep into your eyes. As all of heaven's court stands at attention, He announces:

Well done, good and faithful servant.

The words penetrate you to the core, and you sense that they will light your countenance through all eternity.

Then He smiles at you. It's a look of affirmation worth more than the collective achievements of all of humanity's highest accomplishments, more deeply honoring than a million stadiums of standing ovations. He opens His mouth and the words bathe you in brilliant light, soaking you to your grateful core.

Enter into the joy of your master.

Lord, You know me best. You see me chasing after lesser loves, and I want to pursue the higher goal of Your smile at the Judgment Seat of Christ. I desire to orient my whole life toward Your pleasure. I confess I haven't given much thought to Your promise of reward and have brushed away Your honor—what folly! Deliver me from any sense of entitlement that has seeped into my soul, where I would believe that I am above Your evaluation. Ground me in the fear of the Lord. Teach me to number my days, as the Psalmist said, that I may gain a heart of wisdom. I am humbled and amazed that You will reward me for how I live my life before You. Above all else, I desire to hear You say, "Well done, good and faithful servant" on that awesome Day. May my life please You greatly, Lord, even daily. You are worthy of all my attention, affection and adoration. Amen.

CHAPTER TWO

A HOUSE TESTED

His eyes are like blazing fire.

- Revelation 19:12a

As they walked along the bizarre landscape of the debris strewn beach together holding hands, my parents tried to keep themselves from crying. They willed themselves to just keep walking, just keep hoping.

Earlier that morning the Jackson County sheriff's department had allowed residents of Belle Fontaine Beach to go back to their homes—or at least what was left of them. Category 5 Hurricane Katrina had demolished most of these beautiful beach homes a few days earlier, leaving behind only broken foundations and twisted pilons jutting out of the ground. The remnants and rubble were a strange juxtaposition against the unbroken view of the peaceful Mississippi Sound.

My parents carried cardboard boxes in case there was anything left to salvage, but as they passed grieving neighbors sifting through their own wreckage, they feared that their boxes, too, would be empty. All those photographs, all those paintings, all those keepsakes were most likely gone.

In the years leading up to their retirement, my parents had been meticulous in planning and saving for their dream home—a two-story, 3,000-square-foot architectural beauty designed with their two kids and seven grandkids in mind. It would be a comfortable place with lots of bright areas to sit and read in front of large windows facing the gulf, and a footpath leading to the beach that beckoned their grandkids into fun and adventure.

The dream beach house was quite a spread for a couple of people who had grown up in poverty in lower income areas of New Orleans. Neither had graduated high school but both worked hard at service industry jobs. They met each other when they were working at the same hotel in the French Quarter, my dad as the night auditor and my mother as a cashier at the hotel's restaurant.

They got married, had my sister and me, and continued to work diligently at their jobs, getting enough promotions along the way to lift our family to the level of a middle-class American lifestyle. As my sister and I transitioned into our adult lives, their increase in disposable income went into building their dream house.

Their dream succeeded. The beach house was a magical and memorable place for their extended family and a constant in my own young family's life as traveling missionaries home on furlough. Playing "Survivor" games on the beach organized by my creative mother. Exploring trails that ran along the nearby bayou. Eating dinner together on the porch with a vivid sunset as a backdrop. The kids making plays and puppet shows for their adoring grandparents before bedtimes.

Now was all of that gone?

They continued walking along the beach, careful to avoid sharp objects, heartbroken for their neighbors' demolished houses and marveling at the strength of the hurricane. Wreckage was strewn even high into the surrounding pine trees that survived, evidence of the high storm surge.

As they got closer, they looked ahead and saw one house standing in the distance. It looked like it was in half-decent shape. A few more plodding steps through the deep sand made their hope soar. Their house seemed to be still standing!

Tears of grief were quickly replaced by tears of joy as they jumped up and down with their empty cardboard boxes. Later they would learn that, of the 53 houses along the Belle Fontaine Beach of Ocean Springs, Mississippi, 49 were completely swept away. Theirs was one of the four standing with enough structural integrity to warrant a rebuild.

As they got close enough for a better inspection, they saw that their beloved house was significantly damaged but still structurally intact. The storm had gone through the house and randomly sliced up most rooms. The downstairs garage was completely wiped clean, storage boxes and random collectibles all swept away at sea. Half of the master bedroom walk-in closet was gone, with clothes hanging on the other side seemingly untouched. One wall was torn down and the other wall still had undisturbed dishes inside the cabinets. Their baby grand piano was upside down on the sand about 100 yards away from the house. Upstairs there was a glass of unfinished wine resting peacefully next to an untouched record player. Eerie and surreal.

Later, a structural engineer would certify the house as rebuildable, and the insurance company would debate whether the damage was wind or water related. It took years, but they were able to rebuild, and we had many more years of family memories there.

Every one of those houses looked strong from the outside, silent sentries overlooking the Gulf of Mexico, yet no one knew how strong they actually were until Hurricane Katrina tested each one. I'm sad for the people who lost their homes, many of them not getting much from the insurance companies due to the inscrutable intricacies of their policies. I'm so glad that my parents had built with the very best materials. During the building stage of their dream house, when my dad was presented with different choices of building supplies, he always went with the highest quality. Their house was built with care, and as Hurricane Katrina was later to attest, it was built to last.

Structural Integrity

There is a storm coming to test the structural integrity of our lives. Unlike a hurricane, which may or may not even appear during an active hurricane season, we know for sure this one is coming.

It's powerful. It packs more punch than a category five storm that can level a row of beach houses and flood an entire city. This storm has enough power to debase all the pride of men through all human history. No president, king or even dictator would ever dare stand in its presence.

Its power is precise. A storm's fury may be indiscriminate, ripping up houses randomly, but this one tests each structure equally. It can even peer between good and bad intentions of the human heart, seeing into the deepest motives of all of our decisions:

Nothing in all creation is hidden from God's sight. Everything is uncovered and laid bare before the eyes of him to whom we must give account. (Hebrews 4:13)

It's penetrating. There is no shielding from its testing nor sidestepping around its thorough examination. This gaze has the absolute right to evaluate us, and no one in that moment would dare open his mouth, try to object on some technicality, utter any excuse or protest in the presence of its holy and awesome majesty.

It's the fire in the eyes of Jesus at the Judgment Seat of Christ.

Fiery Proof

Paul unpacks what this sobering experience will be like in his first letter to the Corinthian believers, in a section where he corrects their fickle frivolity in pitting one spiritual leader against another. He argues each of us will give account of our own lives before God, using the metaphor of an experienced builder laying a solid foundation, then constructing on top of it a building which will later be tested by an intense fire:

By the grace God has given me, I laid a foundation as a wise builder, and someone else is building on it. But each one should build with care. For no one can lay any foundation other than the one already laid, which is Jesus Christ. If anyone builds on this foundation using gold, silver, costly stones, wood, hay or straw, their work will be shown for what it is, because the Day will bring it to light. It will be revealed with fire, and the fire will test the quality of each person's work. If what has been built survives, the builder will receive a reward. If it is burned up, the builder will suffer loss but yet will be saved—even though only as one escaping through the flames. (1 Corinthians 3:10-15)

Paul's audience would have been very familiar with the destruction and devastation of fire. An awful event, probably told from generation to generation, took place 200 years before they received Paul's epistle. The prominent city of Corinth was completely destroyed by a Roman rampage. Soldiers of the Empire slaughtered all the men, enslaved the woman and children, plundered the city and set every structure on fire. Only the finest materials survived the cruel blaze. All of the wooden structures were incinerated, leaving only piles of ash behind.

That devastating fire set a line that still divides the historical monuments of Corinth into the pre-Roman and the ones constructed after the time of Christ. Today, the only pre-Roman ruins that have survived are the ruins of an archaic temple situated on the small hill of the Agora, something made of precious stones. In the Corinthians' collective memory, they would know how devastating a fire could be, consuming everything in its path that is not the highest of quality: gold, silver and costly stones. Everything else was completely gone and unremembered.

Paul ties this analogy of a testing fire to "the Day," the awesome Judgment Seat of Christ which brings the quality of every building to light.

Foundation First

The first thing Paul talks about in his analogy is the foundation, which of course an expert builder would lay down first. This is really good news for us: our lives are built on the foundation of God's amazing grace.

As I mentioned in the first chapter and want to almost over-emphasize in a book on God's judgment, our relationship with God is one hundred percent dependent upon His grace, revealed in Jesus Christ and manifested at the Cross. Jesus Himself laid down the foundation of your house of faith when He laid down His life. Our Savior endured that Cross, despising its shame, and for the joy set before Him brought you to the Father (Hebrews 12:2). As a result, for every blood-bought believer, our sins—past, present and future—have been covered.

Nothing is ever going to change that. No matter what the testing reveals about the structure on top, the foundation underneath remains. "For no one can lay any foundation other than the one already laid, which is Jesus Christ," Paul assures us (1 Corinthians 3:11). I'm so grateful that Jesus Christ is that foundation and not our own works of righteousness.

That grace protects us from the wrath of God, a very real thing:

> But God demonstrates his own love for us in this: While we were still sinners, Christ died for us. Since we have now been justified by his blood, how much more shall we be saved from God's wrath through him! (Romans 5:8-9)

By the grace of God, through the belief in the death, burial and resurrection of Jesus, we are rescued from the dreadful wrath of God. Our names, praise God, are now written in the Lamb's Book of Life (Revelation 13:8 and Revelation 21:27).

The Judgment Seat of Christ is different from the White Throne Judgment of Revelation Chapter 20, when God separates those who have their names in the Book of Life and those who don't. Sobering stuff:

> Then I saw a great white throne and him who was seated on it. The earth and the heavens fled from his presence, and there was no place for them. And I saw the dead, great and small, standing before the throne, and books were opened. Another book was opened, which is the book of life. The dead were judged according to what they had done as recorded in the books. The sea gave up the dead that were in it, and death and Hades gave up the dead that were in them, and each person was judged according to what they had done. Then death and Hades were thrown into the lake of fire. The lake of fire is the second death. Anyone whose name was not found written in the book of life was thrown into the lake of fire. (Revelation 20:11-15)

If you are standing before God at this White Throne of Judgment, being judged by your works and without the mercy as appropriated by the blood of Christ, you are in trouble. The universal reality of humanity is "all have sinned and fall short of the glory of God" (Romans 3:23a), and none of us through our own good works can make up for all that sin. God's perfect holiness demands justice.

Another well-known verse from Romans, often used when describing the Gospel to people who haven't yet believed, is Romans 6:23:

For the wages of sin is death, but the gift of God is eternal life in Christ Jesus our Lord.

For those who trust in Him, God offers eternal life, something that cost Him the greatest sacrifice. He literally paid off the debt of our sins by His death on the Cross, and He was raised to life for our justification (Romans 4:25). Not only are we acquitted at trial, but we are escorted out of the courtroom by the judge himself, who speaks at a press conference afterwards on our behalf to let the world know we are completely absolved of all charges.

What a gift salvation is! The foundation of our life of faith was paid for by Jesus' own blood, a precious sacrifice. I can't emphasize that enough and we will marvel at it throughout all of eternity.

Up to Us

Having established the mind-boggling and soul-altering fact that our life is built on the sure foundation of Jesus Christ, Paul moves on:

If anyone builds on this foundation using gold, silver, costly stones, wood, hay or straw, their work will be shown for what it is, because the Day will bring it to light. (1 Corinthians 3:12-13)

How we build on the foundation of His one hundred percent free grace is one hundred percent in our hands. Paul exhorts, "Each one should be careful how he builds." Just like my dad choosing the very best materials for his dream beach house, a wise builder is thinking of the future and what the elements might do to his structure, not only in the slow wear of time but in a sudden testing like a fire or storm. An expert builder is going to choose the best materials—the gold, silver and costly stones in Paul's metaphor. Those people will be so relieved after the testing that their structures survived.

Leonard Ravenhill, the fiery preacher from the United Kingdom who wrote *Why Revival Tarries*, gave some insight on the difference between the first three building materials and the last three. Gold, silver and costly stones are formed underground where no one can see, he noted, while wood, hay and straw are all found readily above ground.[18]

His point was that the hidden things in our lives—integrity when no one is looking, anonymous giving, our secret prayer lives, sacrificial service unto the Lord and not for the applause of man—are precious to the Lord and will be richly rewarded by Him. We get marked for eternity in the secret place as we reach out to the God of eternity.

Ravenhill wanted to keep this in mind as he went about his days, desiring his life to be oriented toward the applause of heaven. He kept the word "ETERNITY" on signs placed all over his house. It was a word that influenced him throughout his life, and anyone who heard his sermons, read his books or spent time around him could definitely feel that value shining through.

It's stunning to me that how we choose to build upon the foundation of His grace is very much up to us. It's as if God gives us a whole lifetime of white canvas to paint on with the colors of our choosing. We can waste it on the temporary pursuits of pleasure and the fleeting applause of man, and be grieved to find out that the Kingdom impact of our lives is burned up in a millisecond at the Judgment Seat of Christ. Or, by His grace and through abiding in Him, we can create on that canvas a beautiful and colorful painting that will brighten a smile on the face of our King.

What will survive the testing fire of that Day? You and I will be so glad on that Day for every little eternity-oriented choice we made.

Quality Over Quantity

No matter how great of a reputation we acquire or how much our influence grows, the testing on that Day will reveal how much of it was of eternal quality.

...and the fire will test the quality of each person's work. (1 Corinthians 3:13)

Fire tests quality, not quantity. A fire can destroy a very large pile of hay with one tiny diamond hidden inside. If you had to choose, it would be better to have built a smaller house of lasting quality than a larger house of poorer quality, with the view of that fiery testing to come. What counts is what remains.

It's not how much we produce in terms of Gross Kingdom Product that is rewarded, but the quality of our ministry in the lives of people we've impacted. In the Parable of the Talents, the master heartily affirms the servant who had received two talents and made two more, just as much as the one who had received five talents and made five more:

His master replied, "Well done, good and faithful servant! You have been faithful with a few things; I will put you in charge of many things. Come and share your master's happiness!" (Matthew 25:21&23)

The Master's pleasure comes from the quality of the rendered service: "trustworthy with small things." Back to Paul's metaphor, the testing of the structure which leads to reward:

If what has been built survives, the builder will receive a reward. (1 Corinthians 3:14)

These faithful builders at the Judgment Seat of Christ will be affirmed in front of a heavenly audience for their wise choices and will receive their reward. We don't know precisely what those rewards are, but we do know from the scriptures what kinds of things God intends to reward. We see that in the brief descriptions of the crowns Jesus will give out that Day (more on those crowns in Chapters 5-8). We also know that our reward in heaven is going to be more awesome than our human brains could ever fathom on earth, better than the most beautiful dream house on the world's most pristine beach.

Escaping Through the Flames

If it is burned up, the builder will suffer loss but yet will be saved—even though only as one escaping through the flames. (1 Corinthians 3:15)

In the other category are people who are saved, thank goodness, "but only as one escaping through the flames." They got out with their saved souls and nothing else, like grieving beach road residents carrying empty boxes back to their cars, all their belongings and beautiful homes completely wiped away. These believers survived the storm with their lives, and they are sincerely grateful for that, but as Jesus fixes His perfect gaze into their lives, there is nothing left but His grace. As awesome as that grace is, they are shown to have built nothing of lasting value upon it.

What a moment of profound regret that will be! Shocked believers looking into the blameless eyes of Jesus and realizing they have wasted their lives on their own pursuits, with nothing eternal to show for it. Yes, they made it, but barely, with little or no rewards in their hands to lavish back at the feet of Jesus. While others around them are bowing down and basking in His joy, laying their abundant and priceless treasures back at His nail-scarred feet, these self-centered believers only have charcoal in their hands as an offering. Their lives will have been found out to be a squandering of His lavish grace. They are grateful to be there, for sure, but in that moment they would give anything to go back in time and start over, living their entire lives worthy of His glory and gaze.

Does that mean those grace-saved, barely-escaped-the-flames believers will stay mired in regret and not enjoy God forever? No way. Scripture affirms that God will wipe every tear from our eyes (Revelations 21:4), but in that profound moment of regret I imagine there are going to be a lot of tears to wipe away.

A little bit scary? A lot for me. No matter how man evaluates and honors my life, that Day will bring everything to light—

every deed, every thought, every word, even every motive behind why I did what I did. I'm so glad I will be standing on that sure foundation of His grace. But my oh my, how much of what I am doing on earth is for the praise of man?

Jesus warned that the Pharisees had already "received their reward in full" when they made those nice flowery prayers in front of all those impressed people (Matthew 6:5). Ouch. How many times is that me—those little prayers I rehearse in my head before I pray them so they'll sound really good? I'll get zilch from God for every time I did something for religious show. "Wow, that dude sure is spiritual." That's it. The passing thought of a man, worth about as much as used charcoal. And how much of my house is made of charcoal? On His foundation of grace, am I building a palace of hay or a sturdy structure of precious stones?

Only that Day will tell.

That for sure sobers me, but as we end this chapter I want to make the point again that this Judgment Day of Christ is not a matter of separating between evil and righteousness. Again, the debt of our sin was already paid in full at the Cross. This testing is all about proving the quality of our good works, to show reward-worthiness. He intends to severely test because He intends to richly reward.

Aren't you grateful that we have this warning ahead of time? Let's make it our goal to live lives of eternal purpose and have heaps of gold, silver and precious stones to lavish back at the feet of Jesus on that Day. As you peer into His pure eyes of fire, you'll be so glad that you had chosen to build with care.

Lord, thank You so much for the firm foundation of Your grace under my feet. I want what I build on top of that sure foundation to have lasting, eternal value. I know that can happen only through Your grace! O Lord, may the bulk of my life be revealed on that Day before You as gold, silver and precious stones more than wood, hay and stubble. Thank You for the advance notice that my entire life will come before Your pure gaze. I confess that in my day-to-day life I hardly give Your appraisal of me at the Judgment Seat of Christ a passing thought. Change that, Lord. Mark my heart for eternity. Recalibrate my life toward Your smile. Incinerate lesser loves in my life and infuse me with a vision of pleasing You on that Great Day. Amen.

CHAPTER THREE

―――――――

A RAISED PLATFORM

On a long international flight I recently took, I was perusing entertainment options on the seatback screen and this title caught my eye: *Astronauts: Toughest Job In The Universe.*[19] I just had to watch...I mean how can you *not* watch a show with that as the title?

In this reality show, 12 top candidates are chosen out of thousands to go through rigorous astronaut training, and the winner receives a coveted recommendation that all but guarantees he or she gets into the NASA space program as a bona fide astronaut. The head astronaut who does the final recommending is Chris Hadfield, a disciplined man who has had a 30-year career as a fighter pilot and astronaut. He was the first Canadian to walk in space and he flew on two Space Shuttle missions. He served on the Russian space station Mir in 1995 and later served as commander of the International Space Station.

On one of his ISS missions, he became well-known for posting pictures of himself on social media. In 2013, he went out-of-this-world viral (sorry, can't help my dad jokes) when he made the first music video from outer space, singing David Bowie's 1969 hit song *Space Oddity* while floating around and strumming a weightless guitar—a disciplined yet fun guy for sure.

The episode I watched was the grand finale, where Chris chooses between the final three candidates. By this point, they had been pushed well beyond their physical and mental limits over many weeks, with two last hurdles to overcome. The first was riding in the Zero Gravity "Vomit Comet," the nickname for an aircraft that simulates zero gravity (well, technically microgravity, aka 10^{-6} gravity) for about 20 seconds at the top of its parabolic flightpath. In this state of weightlessness, they had to perform a complicated task—install film in a Polaroid camera and take a picture of fellow astronauts with it—all while tumbling around. The second hurdle was performing other more complicated tasks while underwater in a Key West training facility, such as figuring out an air compression sequenced task inside a pressurized and submerged vessel. It's all incredibly complex, and you think after watching it for a while that *yeah, this probably is the toughest job in the universe.*

As they are going through these demanding tests, the producers of the show interview the candidates in short video vignettes. One of them, named Karen, says this with a wide grin:

> Having Chris' backing would be such an honor, and it would almost be like this golden light shining on you. Imagine just thinking that Chris believes in you. That would be incredible.[20]

Through their unimaginably grueling training, arguably to get the toughest job in the universe, one goal kept them going. Whether they were being tested by a challenging task at the NASA training center, competing high up in the "Vomit Comet" in a zero-gravity competition, or troubleshooting deep underwater in a pressurized tank in complicated training exercise, the golden light of this one man's smile would make it all worth it.

The Apostle Paul felt the same desire to please the One whose opinion he most treasured. He understood his life to be fleeting, and at its culmination point he yearned to bask in the golden light of Christ's smile:

> Therefore we are always confident and know that as long as we are at home in the body we are away from the Lord. For we live by faith, not by sight. We are confident, I say, and would prefer to be away from the body and at home with the Lord. So we make it our goal to please him, whether we are at home in the body or away from it. For we must all appear before the judgment seat of Christ, so that each of us may receive what is due us for the things done while in the body, whether good or bad. (2 Corinthians 5:6-10)

The context of this passage is Paul's yearning for heaven. In the preceding verses, he shares about the magnetic pull his soul feels toward eternity, using the metaphor of a person staying in a flimsy tent and longing for a permanent home:

> Meanwhile we groan, longing to be clothed instead with our heavenly dwelling... (2 Corinthians 5:2)

We would prefer to be done with this tent (our earthly bodies) and live in that permanent home (heaven with our new resurrection bodies), but in the meantime our goal remains the same—to please the Lord.

That wasn't a vague wish in Paul's mind that hopefully his life would be pleasing to the Lord in a general sense. His soul pointed like a compass toward a precise, fixed point of evaluation: "For we must all appear before the judgment seat of Christ" (2 Corinthians 5:10). He lived in and for that golden light.

The *Bema*

The Greek word for the judgment seat is *Bema*, which means "raised platform." That phrase may feel kind of bland to us and doesn't mean much, but to Paul's hearers a raised platform packed an emotional punch. The *Bema* in their minds was both a sober seat of judgment and a hoped-for place of honor.

On the judgment side, they would think of it as someone today who is accused of a crime and awaiting trial imagines himself standing before a judge as a defendant or appearing before a tribunal. On the honor side, they would think of it as a modern-day actress would imagine the stage of the Academy Awards and hearing her name called out to come up and receive her long-coveted Oscar.

It was both—a seat of judgment and a bestowment of honor. I want to look at both sides to gain the full impact of the *Bema* on our lives.

A Seat of Judgment

Paul himself, in a story toward the end of the book of Acts, stood before a "raised platform" in the city of Caesarea.

This marvel of a city was built by Herod the Great, the same king that ruled Israel during the time of Jesus. He built this Roman Empire-inspired city, named after Julius Caesar, right on the Mediterranean Sea. It was about 75 miles away from Jerusalem and far enough to get away with bawdy theater and barbaric games that the orthodox Jews would have found loathsome. There was a magnificent stadium facing the sea, which could seat 4,000 spectators, and right above the spot where athletes competed was the *Bema* where King Herod would stand to observe the games, make speeches and confer honor. The athletes oriented their best competition toward that raised platform, much like bands, dancers and singers at the Macy's Thanksgiving Parade would perform their best in front of the televised grandstand on Thanksgiving morning.

In Acts Chapter 23, after an assassination plot against Paul was discovered in Jerusalem, he was transferred to Caesarea in the dead of night. There he was held in prison in Herod's palace for five days while his accusers gathered evidence and traveled from Jerusalem for the trial.

The trial was a complicated legal proceeding, given that it took place over a couple of years in several stages during a transition in power from the reign of Marcus Antonius Felix, the Roman governor of Judea, to Porcius Festus who succeeded him. You courtroom drama lovers (like me) can read the whole thing in Acts Chapters 23-26.

At one point in this multi-phased trial, Paul is standing before Festus. I've underlined where the word *Bema* appears in this text:

And when he had remained among them more than ten days, he went down to Caesarea. And the next day, sitting on the judgment seat, he commanded Paul to be brought. When he had come, the Jews who had come down from Jerusalem stood about and laid many serious complaints against Paul, which they could not prove, while he answered for himself, "Neither against the law of the Jews, nor against the temple, nor against Caesar have I offended in anything at all."

But Festus, wanting to do the Jews a favor, answered Paul and said, "Are you willing to go up to Jerusalem and there be judged before me concerning these things?"

So Paul said, "I stand at Caesar's <u>judgment seat</u>, where I ought to be judged. To the Jews I have done no wrong, as you very well know. For if I am an offender, or have committed anything deserving of death, I do not object to dying; but if there is nothing in these things of which these men accuse me, no one can deliver me to them. I appeal to Caesar." (Acts 25:10-11, NKJV)

That judgment seat was likely the raised platform at the stadium in Caesarea, which still stands today. During public trials, all eyes were fixed on this seat of power, especially those of the accused, as they had the most stake in what was rendered there. No one would dare climb those steps to that raised platform unless they had the proper authority—only the worthy could ascend the steps to the *Bema*.

I imagine Felix seated on a throne and staring down at Paul from that lofty and regal perch with his royal entourage all around him and a large throng of spectators watching with fascination. As the crowd murmurs, I can see Paul looking back up at the *Bema* and fixing his gaze on Felix, the one who had the legal right to sentence him.

Paul knew there was a higher power behind Felix, the Emperor Caesar, to whom he appealed to in that exchange. Yet what gave Paul courage in that moment was that there was an even higher power behind Caesar, the ultimate ruler Jesus Christ, who would be sitting on the ultimate Judgment Seat. He revealed this secret to his believing friends in Corinth years earlier:

I care very little if I am judged by you or by any human court; indeed, I do not even judge myself. My conscience is clear, but that does not make me innocent. It is the Lord who judges me. (1 Corinthians 4:3-4)

The good news for us, gloriously so, is that the One who sits on that Judgment Seat has already taken on Himself the punishment we deserve. Before that *Bema* we are rightly pronounced guilty for the multitude of sins in our lives, yet amazingly the Judge Himself takes on the death penalty for us because He can't bear to see His beloved condemned.

That is the good news of the Gospel. That is why Paul could stand before any human court and be so courageous, knowing that in Christ his ultimate verdict was acquittal.

The *Bema* before the Cross would send shivers down the spines of Paul's hearers. The *Bema* after the Cross filled them with an overflow of gratitude—the worthy one seated on that raised platform had acquitted them with His own blood!

I've heard it said that justice is getting what you deserve, as in you were speeding and a police officer pulls you over and gives you a ticket. Mercy is not getting what you deserve, as in you were speeding and the police officer lets you off with just a warning. But grace, wow, that is some unfathomable stuff. That's getting what you don't deserve, as in you were speeding and the police officer pulls you over, gives you a hundred-dollar bill, smiles, and says have a nice day.

Grace is what's left for us at the *Bema*. Not only are we not sentenced as guilty, but we are honored with rewards.

Charles Spurgeon marveled at both sides of this truth—the freedom from fear of judgment and the expectation of reward at the *Bema*:

> We need have no fear of the judgment to come when we know that we are in Christ, for who fears to enter a just court when he knows that by the highest authority he has already been cleared? How complete the Christian's safety! For there will be no accuser. So bright will be the righteousness of a saint through faith that no accuser will appear...Who, then, need fear to enter the court when every accusation is silenced and a reward is expected?[21]

A Bestowment of Honor

In the culture of the New Testament writers, the Olympic games were a really big deal. Paul's references to Olympic competitions and prizes referred to the Isthmian Games which were held near Corinth.

Just to give you a little taste of their glory and celebration, here's a press release from the Isthmian Games of 196 BC, written by Appian of Alexandria, when the Roman General Titus Flamininus proclaimed the Greek states free from Macedonian hegemony. It's a long story, as you can imagine, but you can get a sense of stadium-filled Olympic celebration in this press blurb:

> When he had arranged these things with them he went to the Isthmian games, and, the stadium being full of people, he commanded silence by trumpet and directed the herald to make this proclamation, "The Roman people and Senate, and Flamininus, their general, having vanquished the Macedonians and Philip, their king, order that Greece shall be free from foreign garrisons, not subject to tribute, and shall live under her own customs and laws." Thereupon there was great shouting and rejoicing and a scene of rapturous tumult; and groups here and there called the herald back in order that he might repeat his words for them. They threw crowns and fillets upon the general and voted statues for him in their cities. They sent ambassadors with golden crowns to the Capitol at Rome to express their gratitude, and inscribed themselves as allies of the Roman people. Such was the end of the second war between the Romans and Philip.[22]

The Olympic Games in Athens, which we are more familiar with because they are the predecessors of our own modern Olympic games, had been going on for hundreds of years in Greece and were well-known throughout Asia Minor by the time Paul wrote his letters. There was nothing more epic in their world than the Olympic Games.

Imagine you are living in an agricultural society, perhaps as a wheat farmer. Your life follows the predictable patterns of sowing and harvest, day after day, year in and year out, all in a never-ending grind. You certainly would perk up with anticipation to briefly escape your drudgery at an exciting athletic event nearby.

What's more, the athletes of these games became local heroes, and they gave it their all preparing for the games, hoping to bring back some hometown Olympic honor.

Just as in today's world, champion athletes received more renown and honor than in just about any other profession. They of course got their bragging rights back then, proving that they were the top athletes of their chosen competitions. But there was so much more.

First, there were some sweet financial rewards for the winners, who paid no taxes for the rest of their lives. No more Grecian 1040 forms to fill out, no more Grecian IRS to deal with, and no more fear of Grecian auditors knocking on their doors. Tax free for life.

They got free lunches down at city hall to boot. How awesome would that be—free gyros for life!

But maybe the most glorious event of all was a parade where the spectators brought the winning athlete home, knocked a big hole in his front wall, and carried him through it to the cheers of all his neighbors. Then afterwards the heralders plugged up that hole with molten metal, a permanent testament to Olympic greatness.

I imagine, years later, people walking by the house with the weird metal glob in the front wall and talking about it:

Hey, whose house is that?

Oh, that's the home of Euripides. Won the 200 Meter back in 12 AD.

You mean Euripides the Rip Tide?

Yep, the very one.

Wow, I can't believe he lives right here. Amazing. Hey, let's go knock on his door.

No way, he probably gets bothered all the time.

Come on, let's get an autograph. My grandfather would be so thrilled.

You get the picture. Obtaining Olympic honor was a really, really big deal in that day. I'm sure Olympic hopefuls envisioned all these perks and honors as they woke up early to train and practiced hard for their upcoming events.

Champions were not awarded gold, silver and bronze medals as they are today. In that era, victors were crowned with an olive branch laurel wreath. It wasn't just any old olive wreath, though, but one handcrafted from a branch of a wild olive tree that grew on Mount Olympus. A boy, whose parents both had to be alive, was chosen to cut down those branches with a sickle made of gold. Then he took the branches to a temple for consecration.

At the temple, the priests would fashion the branches and leaves into semicircles and consecrate them before their gods. Next, these wreaths would be moved with care to the site of the Olympic competition and placed on a gold-ivory table created just for that purpose. There the laurel crowns sat, treated with the same care as an Olympic torch or medal would be treated today, waiting for the head judge to stand on the *Bema* and bestow the honor they represented upon the victors.

It was a dramatic scene, met with thunderous applause at the stadium, when the Olympic judge atop the *Bema* announced the victor's name, picked up a consecrated laurel crown off the gold-ivory table, descended the steps and placed it on the head of the victor. A true crowning moment.

Now read this verse again with a fuller understanding of the honor of the *Bema*:

> For we must all appear before the judgment seat of Christ, so that each of us may receive what is due us for the things done while in the body, whether good or bad. (2 Corinthians 5:10)

We are meant to be stirred by the immense honor of this moment, and for it to influence the "things done while in the body," namely, how we spend our time.

The Worthy Versus the Pointless

I'm making the point that the Cross saves us from the judgment side of the *Bema* and brings us to the honor side. We're saved by grace and from that certainty we are meant to be motivated to receive the honor that will be bestowed on that Day, just as a modern Olympic athlete would be motivated by having the gold medal placed around his neck on the Olympic platform. That being said, you may be wondering about the "good or bad" part of this verse:

> ...that each of us may receive what is due us for the things done while in the body, whether good or bad. (2 Corinthians 5:10)

Will punishment come into play at the Judgment Seat of Christ? Will we receive our "due" for the things done which were bad? Good question.

The word for "good" in this verse is the Greek, *agathos*, which means "of good constitution or nature." Here is some further unpacking of this word from my favorite Bible website, *Blue Letter Bible*:

- of good constitution or nature
- useful, salutary
- good, pleasant, agreeable, joyful, happy
- excellent, distinguished
- upright, honorable[23]

It's the good stuff, meaning the beneficial and honorable. It's spending your life on advancing God's Kingdom and serving others more than simply avoiding sins.

Compared to the "good constitution or nature" of good, Paul talks about the "bad," which is the Greek word, *kakos*. As placed here next to *agathos*, it has more to do with something that has a bad nature, "not such as it ought to be." In other words, worthless. It's the hay and stubble that will get burned up, those things which have no lasting value.

Woodrow Kroll writes about how Paul used the word "bad" in this passage:

…he did not use the usual words for bad. Rather he used a word that does not imply ethical or moral evil, but rather a sense of good-for-nothingness or worthlessness. The judgment seat is where our works for the Lord will be closely scrutinized to see if they are valid or not, acceptable or not. The Judge is concerned with what sort of work we have done, what sort of life we have lived as a Christian servant.[24]

The essence of this verse is not about punishment (I keep saying this because I want to make 100% sure we get it) but about dividing the beneficial from the worthless.

With that Day in mind, Paul is saying we should live for the beneficial good and not the worthless bad, because we will be handsomely rewarded for the former while the latter will burn to ashes.

I remember as a boy when I would clean up my room, or maybe take on an extra task like organizing the clutter in the garage. The whole time I would imagine my parents' faces when they got home from work. They would be so happy! They would be so proud of me! All this mucking around in this dirty garage was going to be worth it because they were going to appreciate and affirm me.

Now I could have spent that day wasting my time playing video games (which I did a lot on my beloved Atari 2600). When my parents came home on those days, there was nothing to punish—I didn't do something they commanded me not to do, but there also would not be anything to reward. I spent my day on a worthless (yet fun) pursuit.

The *Bema* is meant to motivate us toward pursuing worthwhile things and de-prioritizing worthless ones, because the smile on His face will be so worth it all. Remember, Jesus on that raised platform is looking for that which He can reward. That Day will show clearly how we honored Him with our limited time, without any fear of punishment.

In our lives, I'm hoping we spend more time cleaning out the garage than playing the Atari 2600. My prayer is that we would become more like servants than consumers, choosing more challenging Kingdom work over empty and vain pursuits. May our lives be marked for eternity over entertainment.

A life oriented toward the golden light of Jesus' smile will be handsomely rewarded in heaven on that raised platform, more than we can even imagine now, and I dare say will also lead to a life of much richer fulfillment on earth.

Lord, when I imagine You seated on the Bema on that Great Day, I confess that my heart is full of apprehension. I am so aware of all my stubborn struggles and repeated failures. I feel like such a mixed bag of motives, even on my best day, and I wonder what lasting things from my life will be rewarded by Your hand. But I look to You, O Lord. You who began a good work in me will be faithful to complete it. You are transforming me in the favor of Your grace day by day. It is You who works in me to will and to act according to Your good purpose. I want to be ready on that Day and bring a smile to Your face with the way I lived my life. Please deliver me from all my sins, addictions and worthless pursuits, so my life's net gain won't go up in smoke. Pull me out of the stupor of small and petty things. Help my heart to forgive and not to hold on to bitterness. Strengthen me in the disciplines of the secret place. O God, set me ablaze now with the golden light of Your smile!

CHAPTER FOUR

THE CROWN OF AWKWARDNESS

During my senior year of high school, the administration made a decision that the student body would no longer be electing Prom King and Queen. Instead, the teachers and staff would be making that selection themselves. The rationale was they didn't want that coveted spot to be a popularity contest, since that already happened every year in the yearbook's Who's Who pages...Best Dressed, Best Looking, Best Personality, and of course at the apex of high school glory, Mr. and Mrs. Ocean Springs High School. That year, the choosing of Prom King and Queen would be a direct assault on shallow popularity and instead exalt studiousness.

The decision was met with overall ambivalence by the student body. *Okay, whatever, for this year it's gonna be Teacher's Pet Prom King and Queen.* The only consternation I imagine was for Mr. and Mrs. Ocean Springs High School, who probably thought they were dead ringers for this last shot at immortal high school royalty.

I took my girlfriend Stephanie to this senior prom, which had the theme of *Night of Enchantment*, but by the end it turned into the *Night of Awkwardness*.

I must set some context first. The year before, I had dated a girl named Marcia who was on the high school newspaper staff with me, both of us serving as co-editors of *The Hound's Tale* during our junior and senior years. When our relationship started during the fall semester of our junior year, we flirted and made googly eyes at each other as we churned out *The Hound's Tale* week after week. But things soon got choppy, and we broke up by the beginning of the spring semester. We continued to do our journalistic duty, albeit somewhat awkwardly, and *The Hound's Tale* kept the student body informed with its hard-hitting pieces like updates on the parking lot expansion and my own movie review column. That April I started dating Stephanie and asked her to the junior prom.

Flash forward to senior prom. By then I had been dating Stephanie for a year, so we were bona fide high school sweethearts. We had a great time and the evening was really magical, living up to its expectations of enchantment. The grand finale of the event was the pronouncement and crowning of Prom King and Queen for 1988. In the moments leading up to the announcement, it occurred to me that, wait a minute, I actually had a shot at bringing home the crown. Ain't no way I would have won if the students were voting, but in the middle-aged estimation of the teachers who were doing the choosing, I was a pretty likeable and diligent student. Not only that, but the paper staff sponsor, Ms. Van, was the chairperson of the prom committee, and I had made a good impression on her after four years in her journalism class.

That would be so hilarious if they elected me Prom King! Take that, popular kids.

But wait, if they elected me King, does that mean for Queen they would choose...wait, no...

The announcement rang out from the stage, spotlights whirling around the room. "Your Prom King and Queen for Ocean Springs High School, Class of 1988 are…"

God, please no.

"…Mike O'Quin and Marcia Cur…!"

I glanced at Stephanie whose face had turned as red as my rented cummerbund. I'm sure the moment was just as awkward for Marcia and her date, too. In obedience to the summoning, we exes gingerly made our way to the front, and the students who knew the situation thought it was hilarious. "Dance! Dance!" I heard some of those so-called friends shout out hysterically.

We climbed the stairs to the platform, and what transpired next was the most awkward coronation ceremony in history. I received the Prom King crown and Marcia received her Prom Queen crown from the high school principal as Mrs. Van stood on stage and beamed. It was a crowning moment for her, I'm sure. Not so much for us and our dates.

There was a mix of applause, with the faculty cheering loudly and light applause coming from the student body. The legit popular people watched the proceedings with icy stares.

We then descended from the stage and were ordered to take a picture, and you can see some serious space between us in that photo…we were socially distanced before that was even a thing. After the photo shoot, I got that crown off my head as quickly as possible and we made our way back to our prom dates, continuing to ignore my friends' shouts to dance as newly coronated King and Queen.

How embarrassing! Mrs. Van, how could you do this? Don't you know us and realize how awkward this is?

When I got home, I hid that crown in my closet. It stayed there under a pile of other random things, and eventually I threw it out (but I will say for the record that I did hang on to my prom date—from high school sweethearts through courtship in college to 29 years of marriage and counting).

That Prom King crown was not something I was proud of, but more of a reminder of a very awkward moment. While it was in my ownership, I can't remember ever digging it out of my closet and showing it to anybody.

Crowning Glory?

Come to think of it, I can't recall ever being excited about the prospect of receiving a crown. There hasn't been one time in my entire life when the thought of wearing one inspired me toward anything at all.

I get it. Crowns don't do much for us these days. They are not something that motivates us on a typical day, as in, "Honey, I know we've sacrificed a lot for this startup business, but one day we will wear a crown in front of all of our friends!" Culturally for us, crowns feel kind of hokey, like my Prom King story or maybe a kid in Burger King wearing one of those colorful cardboard crowns and feeling so proud of himself.

Yet the Bible is holding out this staggering promise of wearing a crown one day in heaven, with the assumption that imagining that crowning moment would motivate deeper love for Jesus and greater service to people.

Paul's audience was in awe of crown bestowing. So, when he wrote something like this in one of his letters...

Everyone who competes in the games goes into strict training. They do it to get a crown that will not last, but we do it to get a crown that will last forever. (1 Corinthians 9:25)

...they would think, "How awesome is that! I mean, can you imagine receiving a crown, much less one that lasts forever??!!"

For us, not so much.

So how do we get from there to here? How do we tap into the power of the majesty of that moment?

Dynamic Equivalence Theory

Missionary Bible translators run into problems when they try to translate certain scriptural concepts if the culture they're working in has no cultural equivalents of those concepts. For instance, take a lamb. Even though most of us aren't farmers or shepherds, we know what a lamb is—an innocent-looking baby sheep. We've seen films with lambs in them, or maybe have touched one at a petting zoo. Then we come to a passage in the Old Testament about a blameless lamb being brought to the temple to be slain for the forgiveness of the person offering it. We get it...a sacrifice has to be spotless like that innocent little lamb, something we have encountered before. And then we read in the New Testament that Jesus is the perfect, sinless Lamb of God and we get that, too. We think, "Wow, thank You Jesus that You were innocent like a spotless lamb, yet You still voluntarily went to Your own slaughter. Thank You for the Cross, Lamb of God!"

Let's say you're a Bible translator serving among the Inuit people of the Canadian Arctic, where the word "lamb" is non-understandable and evokes no emotions about innocence, or anything else for that matter. Instead of teaching them what a lamb is first before you present Bible passages on this metaphor of innocence, you could take a linguistic shortcut under Dynamic Equivalent Theory, and look around for a dynamic equivalent of something in that culture that is blameless and innocent. [25]

You find out that a seal is innocent and an integral part of their culture, and so you translate Jesus the "Lamb of God" to Jesus the "Seal of God," something that sounds strange to us but for them would be deeply meaningful.[26] The Inuit then would experience Jesus in the same way as a first-century Jewish person would encounter the Lamb of God. You can imagine that this theory is controversial and debated among linguists and Bible scholars.

But let's say for argument's sake you are on board for Dynamic Equivalency Theory and we come to the word "crown." Again, crowns don't do much for us. Don't want one. Would feel extremely embarrassing to wear one in public. Not motivated at all to wear a crown unless you were hallucinating and thought you were the Queen of England. Let's do a Dynamic Equivalency Theory switcheroo and pick something in our culture that would carry with it the same emotional import.

For example, you're a hard-working musician, dreaming of the day when you hold up a Grammy from the stage and thank the Recording Academy for the immense honor. With tears of joy streaming down your face, you mention with gratitude the significant people who helped you along the way to your musical dreams.

Or you're a writer deep in research and plowing through the revising of your long manuscript, imagining the day you might win a Pulitzer Prize.

Or you're a scientist who has spent your life working tirelessly to cure one of humanity's ills, and colleagues are starting to say you may receive a Nobel Prize for your life's work. You imagine being called to the stage in Oslo, Sweden to receive the honor of your life.

Or you're an actor on the set of a prestigious movie, thrilled to get the role of a lifetime. You can't help thinking of the day you might be called to the stage of the Academy Awards. A renowned actor tears open an envelope and utters the longed-for phrase, "And the Oscar goes to..."

Or you're an athlete. You practice and compete hard, dreaming of the day you'll hoist a championship trophy over your head as the confetti rains down.

This is the kind of motivation that a crown is supposed to conjure up for us. World Cup trophy. Stanley Cup. Super Bowl Ring. Cutting down the net at the NCAA Final Four tournament...that kind of thing.

That celebratory and champagne-spewing locker room is worth a season of hustle for hard-working athletes. On early mornings when they don't feel like leaving their comfortable beds and begin training on cold mornings, that imagined scene motivates them to get moving.

We may have to detach ourselves from a modern-day connotation of crown wearing and get back to the first-century motivation for receiving a crown. In essence, a crown is a highly esteemed honor, one given out by the highest authority and worth a lifetime of hard work.

That's what you're going for.

A Greater Race

What falls short in my dynamically equivalent definition, however, is that these more-relatable glories on earth are mere shadows, tin trinkets really, of the awesome honor of receiving a crown in heaven. That permanent honor reveals God's pride and pleasure in you.

The athlete Eric Liddell understood the difference between temporary trophies on earth and permanent crowns in heaven. He was a runner from Scotland whose life was depicted in the 1981 Oscar-winning film, *Chariots of Fire.*[27]

Liddell was raised by missionary parents in China who encouraged his aptitude for running. He carried with him their strong work ethic and religious convictions, including one that forbade any kind of work or competition on the Sabbath. That wasn't much of a problem throughout his days as a top-notch runner at the University of Edinburg, but it did pose a challenge upon graduation when he qualified for the 1924 Summer Olympics in Paris. His conviction led him to skip out on running in the favored 100 meters race because it was held on a Sunday. Instead, he competed in the 400 meters race which was held on a weekday, and he still took home the gold medal.

The next year he returned to China, this time as a missionary teacher. He served kids there wholeheartedly, running a Sunday school and designing a sports stadium in the city of Tientsin.

He met his wife Florence there, and they kept serving in China into the 1930s, when Japanese aggression was growing in the region. For safety's sake the young couple, who then had two young daughters, were sent to serve in a more rural community. In 1941, the British government advised all British nationals in

China to return home as fighting intensified, and a newly pregnant Florence came back home to Scotland with their two daughters.

Eric stayed on to help provide medical treatment and food during the escalating crisis. When the mission compound was overrun by Japanese troops, he fled but was eventually captured and detained in an internment camp. He tried to shine a little light in this oppressive place, organizing games, teaching children and serving the elderly. A fellow prisoner wrote that Eric "was overflowing with good humor and love of life."[28]

He developed a brain tumor and died in the camp in February of 1943 at the age of 43. Five month later, American paratroopers liberated the camp.

What was the secret of the "Flying Scotsman" and faithful saint, whose life was marked by joy, even amid the difficult trials he walked through? In his own words:

It has been a wonderful experience to compete in the Olympic Games and to bring home a gold medal. But since I have been a young lad, I have had my eyes on a different prize. You see, each one of us is in a greater race than any I have run in Paris, and this race ends when God gives out the medals.[29]

When God gives out the medals. That's what Liddell's eyes were trained on, even as he trained for the Olympics. Throughout his obscure service and difficult trials in China, that's the prize he most desired, pleasing the ultimate Olympic Judge who would be waiting for him with a smile and a medal at the finish line.

Eric Liddell is one of the few mortals who have gotten a taste of Olympic glory on earth, so he is an authority on the subject. For him the Olympic torch didn't hold a candle to the glory in store for those who have run faithfully in what he called "the greater race."

Jesus is standing just beyond the finish line of your life, and He is looking forward to placing a crown on your head at the *Bema*. There is no honor on earth that could remotely touch the glory of that moment. When He tells you "Well done," there is no higher authority who could ever add to or overturn that affirmation, throughout all of eternity.

Still Squirming

I feel two things when I think about being rewarded by Jesus.

The first is deeply honored. A verdict of "Well done, good and faithful servant" from His lips would be the ultimate affirmation, worth a lifetime of devotion and service to Him. That imagined scene stirs my soul profoundly.

The second feeling, though, is one of squeamishness. The Worthy One declaring that I am worthy of honor? How could anyone standing in that place, where all arrows of attention point toward Jesus, have even one arrow pointing back at himself?

Does being honored by Jesus make you sort of cringe, some leftover guilt from some sermon you heard about not "touching the glory"? Isn't God very jealous about His glory and won't allow anyone to intrude into it?

Yes, God sits alone at the top of the universe. And He is jealous, in the sense that His heart breaks over false worship and He's angry at what it does to us. But that doesn't mean He's selfish. Theologian and prayer champion Steve Hawthorne explains this in my favorite article of his, "The Story of His Glory": "God is so rich in glory that He bestows extravagant honors upon his human servants without compromising His own majesty in the slightest."[30]

Glory isn't a stale, religious artifact that is kept away from the public in a museum in heaven behind bulletproof, stained glass. Glory is the generous Master of the banquet toasting His honored guests. As we focus our life's gaze on Him, the best part of us—our glory—grows and glows. His glory is reflected in our lives, like a full moon that is not shining out its own light but reflecting the brightness of the sun.

As Paul put it to the believers in Corinth, "And we all, who with unveiled faces contemplate the Lord's glory, are being transformed into his image with ever-increasing glory, which comes from the Lord, who is the Spirit" (2 Corinthians 3:18). Deeper contemplation of Him equals ever-increasing glory for us, meaning the best of us being revealed and celebrated.

Hawthorne explains this uncomfortable, yet deep-down-we-know-it's-true concept further:

There is something deeply satisfying about celebrating someone or something of worth along with others. Perhaps the only thing we find even more satisfying is to be the object of praise and celebration. We are formed with an intrinsic yearning, an essential desiring, to be named, to be recognized, to be loved. This yearning for glory is the hunger that drives us.[31]

Heaven recognizes this yearning and beckons us with the astounding promise of glory *from* God. The faultless Judge who sees it all, right down to the secret heart motivations, is saying don't seek after the temporary glory from man, but rather "seek the glory that comes from the only God" (John 5:44). The key word here is *from*...as in seeking glory from God.

Wait, what? You are telling me to seek glory from God?

Exactly. And if this helps to overcome uneasiness with this truth, try to juxtapose the fleeting glory of man against the eternal glory of God. As I mentioned in Chapter One, Jesus taught us not to settle for a lesser glory on earth as the religious higher-ups of His day did, practicing their acts of righteousness to be seen by men, but rather keep our focus on the Generous Host in heaven who does the ultimate rewarding. In His Sermon on the Mount, Jesus warned against doing secret things like giving, praying and fasting with the public's admiration in mind. "If you do, you will have no reward from your Father in heaven" (Matthew 6:1). How very, very sad.

Those same secret practices, if done with the audience of heaven in mind, get richly rewarded. "Then your Father, who sees what is done in secret, will reward you" (Matthew 6:4). How very, very exciting.

So yes, by all means seek glory *from* God! And if I may be so bold, seek praise *from* God while you're at it, too.

Before you throw this book into the fire for heresy, hang with me through a couple more passages to bring this point home.

Paul wasn't looking for praise from people because he knew God sees everything rightly and would judge him accurately one day. Affirmation from God as judge was his goal:

It is the Lord who judges me. Therefore, judge nothing before the appointed time; wait till the Lord comes. He will bring to light what is hidden in darkness and will expose the motives of men's hearts. At that time each will receive his praise from God. (1 Corinthians 4:5)

That's not praise *to* God, that's praise *from* God, as in God praising you. Yes, after all these years of praising God, He will one day praise you. He saw it all. He's proud of you. He wants everyone to know. To deem you as praiseworthy, He will even bestow on eternal crown on you.

To illustrate this same truth point, Jesus once told a story of two men going into a prayer meeting, one of them with his act together and the other a poor beggar, spiritually speaking, before a holy God. The first man prayed a flowery religious prayer which probably impressed the people around him. The second man was too broken to even look up to heaven. He could only beat his chest and cry out with tears, "God, have mercy on me, a sinner" (Luke 18:13).

Jesus told us this story to knock us down from our self-actualized pyramid and to get us to understand this scene from God's perspective. He gives us the verdict that the broken man is the one who went home justified before God. The other man's religion and comparison had inoculated him against even seeing his own destitute need. His prayers went nowhere but into the ears of his listeners.

Then Jesus added the kicker, "For all those who exalt themselves will be humbled, and those who humble themselves will be exalted" (Luke 18:14b).

We look at a verse like this and focus only on the negative—don't exalt yourself and stay humble (which is true). But don't overlook the second half of the statement, where Jesus is holding out the promise of us being exalted. That exaltation (being recognized and affirmed by a holy God) is supposed to motivate us. Jesus for sure blasts corrupt motivation, but He never indicts the core desire we all have to receive honor. That need in your heart to feel honored is not going away anytime soon. He understands how much we long for recognition, and He doesn't slam us for it. Rather, He points it heavenward.

Deep down each one of us wants to be "exalted"—recognized and honored for who we are and what we have done. Being honored by Jesus is the truest honor that you have been seeking your whole life, because what He says about you isn't just another opinion. It's the deepest truth about you and His affirmation will never be taken away. Does that sound a little bit better than fleeting applause?

This is really good news for those of us, make that all of us, who struggle with mixed motives. Even when I do "spiritual things" like preach a sermon, I crave honor from the people who heard it. "Hey, great sermon," I hope to hear them say.

"Oh, no, no, no," I'll respond, "I give all the glory to God." *But yes, yes yes, tell me more.*

All of us desire recognition, from a small pat on the back for a job well done all the way to the full-blown awards ceremony for a great feat. We may occasionally think of how God appraises us, but most of our attention is focused on our projected public image in the mirror. *How am I coming across here? Am I being recognized for my contribution? Do people appreciate me around here?* Jesus said freedom from this tyranny comes from focusing your attention on the Audience of One. Bring your mixed bag of motives to Him!

In holding out the astounding offer of eternal reward to us, God is basically trying to help us stop obsessing so much on temporary trophies (the fleeting approval of man, that job promotion, the MVP award in whatever arena we compete in) and meditate on what matters to heaven. Let's call it the Trophy Exchange Program, where we exchange our honor on earth (temporary trophies) for honor in heaven (eternal crowns). As the evangelist George Bennard put it in his hymn, "The Old Rugged Cross":

And I'll cherish the old rugged cross
Till my trophies at last I lay down
And I will cling to the old rugged cross
And exchange it some day for a crown[32]

I can agree theologically that one day I will exchange my trophies for a crown, but I gotta say it still makes me squirm. Won't we feel embarrassed? When we imagine wearing a crown one day in heaven in front of our loved ones and all the angels and the King of Heaven Himself, it lands for us the same way the Prom King crown landed on my head. It's got to be extremely awkward, right?

In that moment, won't you remember all your shortcomings on earth? Won't you know it's His mercy and grace that got you through? You're only here because in His goodness He drew you to Himself. Sure, you said yes, but that yes feels so puny here. I mean, now that you behold Him in His fully revealed glory, who wouldn't say yes to *Him*?

With all your failures in mind, and fully understanding as never before that all the good things in your life were powered by His abundant grace, how could you possibly wear a crown in this holy and reverent place, in the presence of the King of Kings who bestowed you with that very grace? The One for whom it is written:

> He eyes are like blazing fire, and on his head are many crowns. (Revelation 19:12a)

How could you possibly wear a crown in front of this blazing-eyed, multi-crowned One?

Good question. The short answer is that you won't be able to for long. In the one instance in which we see people wearing crowns in heaven (the 24 elders), notice the very first thing they do:

> Whenever the living creatures give glory, honor and thanks to him who sits on the throne and who lives for ever and ever, the twenty-four elders fall down before him who sits on the throne and worship him who lives for ever and ever. They lay their crowns before the throne and say:

> "You are worthy, our Lord and God,
> to receive glory and honor and power,
> for you created all things,
> and by your will they were created
> and have their being." (Revelation 4:9-11)

They immediately cast their golden crowns, fashioned by the hand of God, right back at His feet. I bet if we could ask them about it in that awesome moment of worship (though we wouldn't dare interrupt), they would say that they were so glad to have something so majestic to offer before Him in adoration.

The crown you will receive from His hand is no craft job, dress-up crown decorated with cheap trinkets. It's an eternal sign of honor from the most high and honorable God, making the highest tokens of honor on earth look like dust at the bottom of a dustpan.

In that moment, I promise you'll want something incalculably worthy to lay down at the feet of the Worthy One.

The Crown Jewels

On a recent trip back to the U.S. from Asia, our family stopped in London and spent a few vacation days sightseeing. I love doing deep dives into history, and one of my favorite places we visited there was the famous Tower of London, a small castle that used to serve as a watch post and prison right on the Thames River. We had gotten there kind of late on a rainy afternoon, but I'm so glad that we had enough time to tour the main sections and especially to see an exhibit known as the Crown Jewels.

The exhibit is inside an ornate historical building that houses 142 royal ceremonial objects that have been in use by the royal family for the last 800 years. After watching a film of these priceless historical treasures, we were carried along on a slow-moving travellator to behold them one by one. The apex of that experience is the coronation section, items used only when a new monarch is crowned.

There we saw the Sovereign's Orb, a symbol of godly power that is placed in the hand of the new reigning monarch by the Archbishop of Canterbury at coronation. This gold sphere is 30 centimeters wide with an ornate cross on top and was crafted in 1661 for the coronation of King Charles II. The orb is mounted with 9 emeralds, 18 rubies, 9 sapphires, 365 diamonds, 375 pearls, an amethyst and a glass stone. Impressive.

Next we saw the Sovereign's Scepter, which represents both the temporal power of the reigning monarch and good governance. The scepter holds the world's largest diamond, the Cullinan I, popularly known as "The First Star of Africa." That beauty is a sight to behold as the largest clear-cut diamond in the world at 530 carats. The placard underneath explains that the diamond was found in South Africa in 1905 by Thomas Cullinan, and that it took 8 months to complete the cutting. It was then gifted to Edward VII in 1907 to help mend relations between Britain and South Africa after the Boer War. But I digress...just take my word for its exquisiteness.

Then there is the final crowning moment on the tour, the actual Coronation Crown, called St. Edward's Crown, after Saint Edward the Confessor. This crown has been used in the coronation of English monarchs since the 13th century. There it was right in front of us, sitting in its solid gold glory and decorated with 444 precious and semi-precious stones. Its ornate beauty is breathtaking.

It's so special, in fact, that at the very end of the tour there is a glass case that holds a special leather case fashioned to perfectly fit around the priceless Coronation Crown and transport it to Westminster Abbey for the next coronation. A case for the case for the crown!

I'm also trying to make a case for the crown here. Seeing all those priceless and precious artifacts, especially St. Edward's Crown, filled me with awe. Even after I had stepped out of the museum and back into the drizzle of London's gray weather that day, I couldn't shake the feeling that I had just beheld some of the world's greatest glories...it's a hard feeling to describe.

Now let's think about heaven and your own crown. It's being designed as you read this. The decisions you are making today, even the smallest ones, are fashioning your crown and the glory that will be emanate from you throughout all eternity.

People joke about "another jewel in my crown" almost dismissively when they talk about doing something noble on earth. We lightheartedly connect a good deed now with honor later. Scripture pushes all kidding aside and affirms this noble truth. One of the 444 gems in St. Edward's Crown would be a tiny piece of tin foil next to the glory of receiving the tiniest sign of honor in heaven. One smile in heaven would be worth more than all of these 142 priceless artifacts put together times a zillion.

Every time you stand strong against temptation and cling to Jesus. Every time you choose the lower road of humility, releasing and forgiving. Every time you serve someone else with a good attitude. Every time you offer a prayer, compassion, the Gospel or a cup of cold water in His Name. Every time you walk through a trial and stay true to Christ. These are the priceless treasures of heaven.

For our light and momentary troubles are achieving for us an eternal glory that far outweighs them all. (2 Corinthians 4:17)

Outweighs them all. Think about that for a minute. Paul is holding up eternal glory as a thing to pursue over all the glories of earth, even if it means momentary troubles or severe hardships. In a place infinitely more glorious than Westminster Abbey, not the lowly-by-comparison Archbishop of Canterbury, but the actual King of Heaven will place a fashioned crown on your bowed head for your life's service to Him, a sign of honor from the most honorable authority that ever existed or will exist.

There could be no more precious treasure than that symbol of how He was honored by your poured-out life, and you get to lay it right back at His feet again.

I'm so grateful that we are given a peek in the Bible of this back-and-forth bestowing of honor, which is the deepest longing in all of us, our true glory. In the next four chapters we're going to look more closely at the four different crowns of the New Testament, each championing a different Kingdom value and each one a testament of how we glorified Him with our lives.

Lord, if am being honest here, and there's no point in not being honest before You, I'm uncomfortable with the thought of receiving any honor from You. I can't seem to shake the feeling that my desire for honor is somehow wrong. Yet Lord, I confess that You know best. You created me and You are familiar with all my ways. You see how I strive so hard and position myself so carefully to receive approval from man. I ask, Lord, that you exchange all those vain pursuits for the higher pursuit of seeking honor from You. I want to have something precious to lay at Your feet in that awesome place, a crown that is worthy of Your glory!

Thank You for this promise of heavenly crowns. Dare I say thank You that one day You will honor me? Anchor me to my truest heart's desire of pleasing You. Let that coming joy be my strength today. Even in the smallest of details and places of obscurity, Lord, orient my life toward pleasing You! King Jesus, I am humbled by any honor you would bestow on me on that Great Day, and may my life be one that honors You daily. Amen.

CHAPTER FIVE

THE CROWN OF GLORY

Be shepherds of God's flock that is under your care,
watching over them—not because you must, but
because you are willing, as God wants you to be; not
pursuing dishonest gain, but eager to serve; not
lording it over those entrusted to you, but being
examples to the flock. And when the Chief
Shepherd appears, you will receive the crown of
glory that will never fade away.

— I Peter 5:2-4

On the Indonesian island of Kalimantan (formerly Borneo), thousands of remote villages are tucked up high in the forbidding interior mountain ranges. People live their whole lives without running water and electricity. There are few books and no theaters or TV, so there are hardly any windows into the outside world. Poverty and sickness are rampant. The only education afforded to most kids is for them to learn the oral traditions of their elders, but not math, science or even the national language of *Bahasa Indonesia* that would help them cope in the modern world. The villagers who are brave enough to make the long trek through the mountains and into the more developed coastal cities encounter a world that they are not prepared for.

Krunani grew up in once such village in the 1970s. Like his friends, he ran around the jungle hunting wild boars with blowgun darts and living a very hand-to-mouth existence with his family. There were no modern conveniences to enjoy nor a school to attend, yet he never felt sorry for himself as he knew no other world to compare to his own experience.

His village life centered around farming, cooking, and the religious requirements of the animistic beliefs that his tribe clung to, in hopes of appeasing the spirits enough to avoid curses.

Unfortunately for Krunani's family, a curse of sorts did fall. A terrible sickness brought 10-year-old Krunani, their firstborn, close to death's door. They upped their religious sacrifices and turned to the local witch doctor, pleading for his supernatural help, but to no avail. Their beloved son was dying on a thatched mat on the dirt floor of their simple home, and there was nothing they could do about it.

Many years later, as a grown man, Krunani told me what happened next. He said his spirit started to slip away and hover over his body. He could see his grieving parents weeping over his lifeless body as he drifted upward. He looked and noticed two enormous, scarred hands lifting him higher and away. Not knowing who this otherworldly being was, he just called out, "Sir, may I get back to my family?" The scarred hands slowly brought him back down to his body below and he quickly recovered.

Life went on in the regular village rhythms until about a year later when his family and the village elders made a decision that would forever alter the course of young Krunani's life. They understood that the kids of the village would have a brighter future if they could leave the remote mountains and go live in the coastal cities. A group of young people was chosen to make the dangerous and long trek through the mountains into one of the coastal cities and make a new life there. Eleven-year-old Krunani was one of the 10 boys chosen. The group survived the weeks-long jungle trek, but they were ill-prepared when they arrived at a highway that led to one of the coastal towns. These innocent children had never seen a TV show and could not have imagined the existence of motorized vehicles. As they heard an ongoing truck barreling up the highway, they scurried back into the thick jungle and away from the terrifying monster!

Eventually they summoned their courage and made it to the city. Miraculously, a group from a Christian church saw these dirty, hungry and barefoot little jungle boys and took them in. They were brought to different houses to figure out what to do next. Krunani was brought to a house which was beside a little church building. As the kind family got him clean clothes and fed him, he looked up at the mural on the church wall next door. It was a painting of two enormous, scarred hands reaching out, and Krunani instantly knew this to be the same majestic being who had healed him. He knew somehow that he was going to be okay.

Later he was officially adopted into this family and was raised as a Christian. He served in that little church as he grew up, and always carried with him a heart for orphan children. Krunani knew firsthand of their pain and how their lives could be turned around by a loving Christian family.

Later in life, Krunani started an orphanage in a small Kalimantan city near the coast. I visited his orphanage of 30 kids several years ago with my daughter Ana when she was still in high school, and we were both amazed at how many kids that Krunani and his kind wife could take care of with so few resources. They themselves lived in a tiny little shack of a house in the middle of the compound while the kids lived in nicer dorms.

Around dinnertime, they asked us if we liked fish and we said sure. Words were called out from their house and a couple of the boys immediately jumped into a stocked pond and caught a few catfish with their bare hands. They chopped them up right in front of us and afterwards we had a hearty meal. The girls whisked Ana away to their rooms, wanting to show her their world. I spent hours late into the night hearing Krunani's story under the light of a solitary lightbulb that hung by a wire over our simple meal. I felt deeply touched by his life of sacrifice to bring all these children up in a loving environment that he and his wife had created. This one little orphanage was the only Christian witness in the Muslim village, a tiny outpost of light that shone brightly. It had a reputation of compassion and the kids growing up inside of it were doing well in the local public school. Krunani and his wife made sure, with the help of a couple of other staffers, that the kids took advantage of the free public education offered to them. Homework every night was required.

We joined them for their 5:00 AM chapel service before they left for school by foot at 6:15 AM. Such joyful singing, waking up the dawn. I know I will never forget their smiles. After they left for school, I discussed ways we could support them with the ministry I represented at the time, Mustard Seed International. Krunani was glad to receive any resources we could offer, as his heart beat for these kids night and day. He wanted them to have a bright future and to bring the Gospel throughout Indonesia after being raised and shaped in a Christ-honoring environment. These children would be the brightest and best as they advanced God's Kingdom in a loving and honorable way.

Our visit soon came to an end but the impact lingered. Ana and I were both inspired by getting to be part of this vibrant and loving community for a few days, led by an unsung hero living his life in such simplicity and joy.

Unsung Heroes Finally Sung

Imagine with me the Great Day of the Judgment Seat of Christ, when it will be revealed to Krunani just how far his impact reached and how much his life touched the heart of God. Though on earth his ministry wasn't fueled or benefitted by prestige, on that Day all heaven will watch with bated breath as the unsung hero is finally sung.

And that song...just one note would be worth a thousand lifetimes of faithful service to the King in total obscurity.

On that Great Day, Krunani will finally hear these words of matchless praise from the pure lips of Jesus: *Well done, good and faithful servant.* And as if that weren't enough, though it would be for any living being past, present or future, the Great Shepherd has one more sign of honor which Krunani will have with him throughout all eternity.

There's something in His hands, the same scarred hands that brought life back to young Krunani's lifeless body and let him know later through a church wall mural that everything was going to be okay. It's something beautiful and precious.

These same scarred hands are now holding a magnificent and unfading Crown of Glory.

Krunani feels shocked to realize that this sign of honor is just for him. He is about to be honored by the great God of heaven and Krunani feels so unworthy of it. Yet knowing how pure and true this Great Shepherd is, it would be a great disrespect to deflect this honor.

The Great Shepherd finally gets to honor one of his favored shepherds, and Krunani receives the priceless and unfading Crown of Glory with surprise and delight. It's a delirious mixture of unbelief and belief. Mostly Krunani is feeling joy. He felt a fair amount of that on earth even on mundane days, but here in this moment his fully ripened joy knows no bounds.

Krunani gathers the courage to look into the Good Shepherd's eyes even as he is being honored. In the reflection of those pure eyes, he sees the faces of the orphans that he has spent his life serving. He feels both an appreciation from Jesus for caring for them and a love for each of their familiar faces. He loved them on earth, imperfectly for sure, but now he sees the source of all that undying love—it was the heart of the Good Shepherd all along. Krunani is being honored for the very love that the Good Shepherd graced him with.

Krunani also sees something else in Jesus' eyes. Joy. It seems that the Good Shepherd has been looking forward to this moment as well.

Close to the Good Shepherd's Heart

There is a special sign of honor in heaven for those who have shepherded well, loving the people under their care not just because of their positional authority over them or the benefits they might receive from that exalted state (status, financial benefits, fame, accolades or perks). Their heart motivation is to care for people as they have been cared for by the Good Shepherd:

> Be shepherds of God's flock that is under your care, watching over them—not because you must, but because you are willing, as God wants you to be; not pursuing dishonest gain, but eager to serve; not lording it over those entrusted to you, but being examples to the flock. And when the Chief Shepherd appears, you will receive the crown of glory that will never fade away. (1 Peter 5:2-4)

Be Shepherds of God's Flock

The Greek word for shepherd is *poimainō,* and according to a Bible dictionary, it means:

> to feed, to tend a flock, keep sheep
> to rule, govern
> to furnish pasture for food
> to nourish
> to cherish one's body, to serve the body
> to supply the requisites for the soul's need[33]

I love that last phrase, to "supply the requisites for the soul's need." There is a nurturing and nourishing sense to *poimainō.* It's more relational than positional. It flows from the heart, just like the love and compassion of Jesus.

And on this Day, Jesus will reward you for the ways His love and compassion flowed from your heart to those whom you shepherded.

That Will Never Fade Away

This verse makes the point that this bestowed crown is a forever one. That's how important this Kingdom value of shepherding is to Jesus, the Chief Shepherd. It will "never fade away," because Christ desires a permanent mark of appreciation for the way His under-shepherds cared for His flock. It's a special honor for those who lean into their role as shepherds, those "eager to serve" out of a sincere love born from His own heart.

We get a great peek into the Good Shepherd's heart in the ninth chapter of Matthew. Jesus has been on a long tour through towns and villages with his disciples, teaching and healing countless people along the way. This scene plays out next:

> When he saw the crowds, he had compassion on them, because they were harassed and helpless, like sheep without a shepherd. (Matthew 9:36)

It breaks the heart of Jesus when He sees people struggling through life on their own without anyone to show them care, comfort and counsel. The next verse shows the Good Shepherd's next move toward the aching cry of humanity:

> Then he said to his disciples, "The harvest is plentiful but the workers are few. Ask the Lord of the harvest, therefore, to send out workers into his harvest field." (Matthew 9:37-38)

We are the answer to that prayer from the compassionate heart of Jesus, sent out with new hearts and restored lives into the lives of the broken. When someone says "Yes" to His heart cry and is willing to be sent out to care for these harassed and helpless people, the heart of the Chief Shepherd brightens. It lights up so much that His eternal delight is eventually forged into the unfading Crown of Glory.

Those who care for others are close to the heart of Jesus, and He wants all of heaven to know. They will be wearing this unfathomably glorious crown as the twinkle of His unending smile. Think of a Sunday school teacher who had an impact on you, a co-worker who offered God's comfort, a Bible teacher who not only taught you God's Word but showed you God's love, a small group leader who listened well, a pastor who lived an authentic life of passion for Jesus and compassion for people. All of that faithful pastoring may not get a lot of flashy fanfare on earth, but it is a really, really big deal in heaven.

Even when it's hard, even when the sheep don't listen, even when they sometimes bite back, Christ beckons these shepherds to release hurts back to Him and forgive again. He restores the hearts of these wounded shepherds and sends them back into His harvest. His song becomes theirs—a love for the harassed and helpless, one that never fades. When our Chief Shepherd sees His under-shepherds pastoring out of His own heart, it pleases Him greatly, and He looks forward to rewarding them with a glorious crown that will never fade.

Lord, I worship You as the Chief Shepherd. Thank You so much for Your heart for us and how You restore our hearts. Thank You that You look with compassion on the harassed and helpless, those sheep without a shepherd. I ask You to use me in Your purposes to bring love and care to the people that You carry in Your heart so deeply. Make me into an under-shepherd who cares for them tenderly and protects them fiercely. Thank You for the promise of the Crown of Glory. O Lord, with Your grace and empowered by Your compassion, I desire to be a candidate for this unfading crown. Send me out as a worker into Your harvest, Lord, and empower me to shepherd the flock You entrust to me with Your unending compassion. Amen.

CHAPTER SIX

THE CROWN OF LIFE

Be faithful until death,
and I will give you the crown of life.

– Revelation 2:10b, NASB

Blessed is the one who perseveres under
trial because, having stood the test, that person will
receive the crown of life that the Lord has promised
to those who love him.

– James 1:12

"Dad, remember the fleas!"

My daughter Naomi recently exclaimed this with a big smile on her face while I was amid a minor inconvenience. I immediately knew what she meant, that I should try to find something to give thanks for and obey the biblical admonition to "give thanks in all circumstances" (1 Thessalonians 5:18a).

Naomi had recently read *The Hiding Place*, the biography of Corrie ten Boom and her experiences of trying to stay faithful to

God in a Nazi concentration camp. The "flea story" in that inspiring book really impacted my daughter.

Corrie was born in 1892 to a watchmaking family in Holland. During the Nazi invasion in World War II, her family hid persecuted Jews in a secret hiding place in their home, believing their Christian duty mandated the risk of protecting Jews. They were caught and arrested for this treason, and Corrie and her sister Betsie were sentenced to the notorious Ravensbrück Concentration Camp north of Berlin. The book details their kindness to other prisoners and their faithfulness to God even amid the savagery of that cruel place. I can see why the story impacted Naomi (that book has stayed with me even though I read it over 30 years ago!).

The flea story comes when Corrie and her sister Betsie were moved to "Barracks 28," a cramped place crowded with hundreds of fellow women prisoners. The squalid barracks were stacked with massive square platforms three levels high that served as bunks, with only enough space between stacks for prisoners to walk through single file. Rancid straw was scattered over the packed platforms, and each one was so close to the other levels that the prisoners could not sit upright on their own platform without hitting their heads on the deck above them.

Even worse were the thousands of fleas swarming the barracks. On one particularly bad day dealing with the vermin, Corrie asked out loud how they could possibly go on living in such a wretched place. Her sister challenged her with the admonition of 1 Thessalonians 5:16-18, to "rejoice always, pray continually, give thanks in all circumstances; for this is God's will for you in Christ Jesus."

"That's it, Corrie! That's His answer. 'Give thanks in all circumstances!' That's what we can do. We can start right now to thank God for every single thing about this new barracks!" I stared at her; then around me at the dark, foul-aired room.[34]

The two sisters went down a list of things to be thankful for even in that miserable place: that they were assigned together, that they had a Bible, and that they had found spiritually open people in the prison. Then Betsie challenged her sister to go a step further and give thanks for the fleas:

The fleas! This was too much. "Betsie, there's no way even God can make me grateful for a flea."

"'Give thanks in all circumstances,'" she quoted. "It doesn't say, 'in pleasant circumstances.' Fleas are part of this place where God has put us."

And so we stood between tiers of bunks and gave thanks for fleas. But this time I was sure Betsie was wrong.[35]

Soon the sisters were holding worship services in the barracks attended by large groups of women under one small light bulb. It became so crowded that they started doing a second service after evening roll call.

Night and day outside those barracks, the prisoners were under heavy surveillance from the guards, with half a dozen continually present. Yet in the large dormitory there was no supervision at all, so they could share freely and boldly with all the other prisoners about the hope that was within them. They could worship their hearts out with no interference. Corrie describes the moment when they figured out why:

> One evening I got back to the barracks late from a wood-gathering foray outside the walls. A light snow lay on the ground and it was hard to find the sticks and twigs with which a small stove was kept going in each room. Betsie was waiting for me, as always, so that we could wait through the food line together. Her eyes were twinkling.
>
> "You're looking extraordinarily pleased with yourself," I told her.
>
> "You know, we've never understood why we had so much freedom in the big room," she said. "Well–I've found out." That afternoon, she said, there'd been confusion in her knitting group about sock sizes and they'd asked the supervisor to come and settle it.
>
> "But she wouldn't. She wouldn't step through the door and neither would the guards. And you know why?" Betsie could not keep the triumph from her voice: "Because of the fleas! That's what she said, 'That place is crawling with fleas!'"
>
> My mind rushed back to our first hour in this place. I remembered Betsie's bowed head, remembered her thanks to God for creatures I could see no use for. [36]

The entire book is such a powerful testimony of these two sisters who remained faithful against the backdrop of a barbaric regime, even giving thanks inside flea-infested barracks. I love stories like these that inspire my daughter and pull me out of my own sense of entitlement and pettiness. Testimonies of faithful saints like Corrie ten Boom who have endured suffering inspire us to live to greater heights.

Of Whom the World Was Not Worthy

Heaven stands to honor the saints who have endured under trial and have remained faithful to their God. He will bestow on them the Crown of Life, an enduring honor that shows up twice in the New Testament, both times for those who have endured a bitter season or who have been faithful, some even until death.

The One described as "a man of suffering, and familiar with pain" (Isaiah 53:3), and who wore a crown of thorns on His way to the punishing Cross, will place the Crown of Life on the head of His fellow suffering servants. I can't imagine a more moving scene.

The first suffering servant we find in the New Testament who is honored by the King of Heaven is a young man named Stephen, a leader in the very first community of Jesus followers. He was taken into custody by envious religious leaders for healing people and preaching the Good News to the people of Jerusalem, some of whom were not ready to hear. He boldly proclaimed the Gospel during his defense before a religious court, starting with the patriarchs and continuing on to the prophets, emphasizing the point that God's people more often than not reject His messengers. This stirred them up into a rage:

When the members of the Sanhedrin heard this, they were furious and gnashed their teeth at him. (Acts 7:54)

The next scene is a breathtaking affirmation from heaven.

But Stephen, full of the Holy Spirit, looked up to heaven and saw the glory of God, and Jesus standing at the right hand of God. "Look," he said, "I see heaven open and the Son of Man standing at the right hand of God." (Acts 7:55-56)

When we see Jesus in almost every glimpse of heaven in the New Testament, He is seated. He's seated among the 24 elders. He's seated on a white horse. He is seated on a throne. But in this case, He is standing! The Son of God is actually standing to honor His servant Stephen during his last moments on earth.

After Stephen says out loud what he is seeing—the Lord Jesus standing at the right hand of God—the crowd flies into a bloodthirsty rage. This blasphemy was too much to take, and they drove him out of the city to hurl stones at him until he died.

While they were stoning him, Stephen prayed, "Lord Jesus, receive my spirit." Then he fell on his knees and cried out, "Lord, do not hold this sin against them." When he had said this, he fell asleep. (Acts 7:59-60)

What an exclamation point at the end of a life lived to the fullest for the glory of the Savior!

Elsewhere in the New Testament, we read about the faithful saints who stood through trial and remained true to the end, those "of whom the world was not worthy" in the translation of the King James Bible. Here is a more modern translation of the same passage from Hebrews Chapter 11:

> There were others who were tortured, refusing to be released so that they might gain an even better resurrection. Some faced jeers and flogging, and even chains and imprisonment. They were put to death by stoning; they were sawed in two; they were killed by the sword. They went about in sheepskins and goatskins, destitute, persecuted and mistreated—the world was not worthy of them. They wandered in deserts and mountains, living in caves and in holes in the ground. These were all commended for their faith, yet none of them received what had been promised, since God had planned something better for us so that only together with us would they be made perfect. (Hebrews 11:35-40)

This is the great hall of fame of faith, and as the writer moves into Chapter 12, he describes a "great cloud of witnesses" almost as a crowd in heaven's grandstands, cheering us on and serving as an example of those who waited for the breakthrough and never saw it with their earthly eyes. They inspire us to remain faithful under trial and to live lives of singular devotion to Jesus.

Crown of Life Heroes in Church History

The great cloud of witnesses rolls on through church history, bringing into its grandstands hundreds of thousands who gave the ultimate sacrifice for the glory of God.

I think of people like **Polycarp**, the second-century bishop of Smyrna who, like the apostle John, lived a long, faithful and fruitful life and fought heresies along the way. For not being willing to offer incense to the Roman emperor as a god, Polycarp was sentenced to death. It is recorded that, on execution day, he said, "Eighty and six years I have served Him, and He has done me no wrong."[37] He was then led to a pile of wood to be burned at the stake and pierced with a spear. At his life's farewell he cried out, "I bless you Father for judging me worthy of this hour, so that in the company of the martyrs I may share the cup of Christ."[38]

I think of people like **John Tyndale** who lived with a passion to disseminate God's Word to the masses. In 1525, Tyndale translated the Bible from Greek and Hebrew into English, printing his work on the breakthrough innovation of the Gutenberg Press. Standing against official church opposition, Tyndale and his partners smuggled the Bibles into England. For this crime, Tyndale was tracked down and burned at the stake in 1536. I imagine that in the blink of an eye after that horrific and painful suffering, he opened his eyes in the splendor, pleasure and wonder of heaven, and soon thereafter was rewarded with the Crown of Life.

I think of long-suffering saints like **Adoniram Judson** who gave their full lives for Christ and His Kingdom through a poured-out life of toil and hardship. Judson was born in 1788 in Malden, Massachusetts, when the United States was a very young country. He gave his life to Jesus after his partying college roommate died, and God lit him up with a fire to reach the unreached. Young Judson set his sights on India, quite a radical decision amid the prevailing theology of the time. He fought against those headwinds and became the very first missionary sent from American soil. When he arrived in India, he discovered that American citizens weren't so welcome because of the United States' conflict with England in the War of 1812. His new mentor, Englishman William Carey, encouraged him to look further east. He moved to Burma with his wife in 1812, and their first child was miscarried on the boat voyage there.

His life of suffering and even torture for the sake of the Gospel in a very tough place has inspired countless people to keep toiling. I read his biography on a plane ride on the way to Myanmar (formerly Burma) recently, and I was moved to tears at the account of this faithful servant. While I was there on this trip with my wife and daughter, I couldn't help feeling the echoes of his faithful testimony to the Burmese people. Judson was buried at sea after dying from a serious lung infection in June of 1850, and a simple tomb in Plymouth, Massachusetts memorializes his life:

Malden, His Birthplace
The Ocean, His Sepulcher
Converted Burmans, And
The Burman Bible His Monument
His Record Is On High[39]

I love that last phrase, "His Record Is On High." That's the one that counts. I imagine Adoniram receiving a Crown of Life at the Judgment Seat of Christ with tears streaming down his overwhelmed face. And I'm sure he would willingly go through another life of suffering and trial to see that same look of joy and honor in Jesus' eyes.

I think of the suffering saints in more recent history, like the German pastor and theologian **Dietrich Bonhoeffer** who was arrested in April of 1943 for speaking bold, biblical truth against Hitler's regime. For a year and a half, he was imprisoned at the Tegel military prison awaiting trial, and even in that squalid place he remained cheerful and had a profound impact on his fellow inmates and prison guards. One of the guards offered to help him escape, but Bonhoeffer declined, fearing retribution against his family.

After a failed assassination plot on Hitler's life in July of that same year, Bonhoeffer was discovered as one of the co-conspirators and was fast-tracked to a concentration camp, where he remained his steadfast and cheerful self. Hitler soon ordered that all the plotters of this conspiracy be killed, and he was sent by dark railway car to a second concentration camp with other prisoners who were condemned to die.

On the morning of his death, April 9, 1945, he led a final Sunday service for his fellow prisoners, and as he was being led to the gallows he is recording as saying, "This is the end—for me the beginning of life."[40] He was then stripped naked and hung, just two weeks before soldiers from the U.S. infantry divisions liberated the camp, and just one month before the surrender of Nazi Germany.

One doctor who witnessed the execution later wrote, "I saw Pastor Bonhoeffer...kneeling on the floor praying fervently to God. I was most deeply moved by the way this lovable man prayed, so devout and so certain that God heard his prayer. At the place of execution, he again said a short prayer and then climbed the few steps to the gallows, brave and composed. His death ensued after a few seconds. In the almost fifty years that

I worked as a doctor, I have hardly ever seen a man die so entirely submissive to the will of God."[41]

I was stirred reading the masterful biography of his life, *Bonhoeffer: Pastor, Martyr, Prophet, Spy.*[42] Bonhoeffer was really all of those things, and the fire that burned in his heart for Christ all his life was greater than the fiery trials that he endured.

There are so many members of this great cloud of witnesses to be inspired by. Don't even get me started on **Jim Elliot**, the young missionary I mentioned in Chapter One, who was speared to death by members of an indigenous tribe in Ecuador whom he was trying to befriend for the sake of the Gospel. His widowed wife, Elizabeth Elliot, eventually moved back to the same tribe with her daughter and brought the Gospel to the very people who had murdered her husband. Her book about her husband's martyrdom, *Through Gates of Splendor,* along with her biography of his life with many of his journal entries, *Shadow of the Almighty*, have moved me deeply. I also recommend the biography Elizabeth Vaughn wrote about her life, *Becoming Elizabeth Elliot*, another heart-stirrer. There is something so rich for the soul when you read of people who were faithful to the end. I often come away from these stories realizing how petty and entitled my comfort-craving soul has become, and how much it needed a good dose of healthy, eternal perspective!

Crown of Life Candidacy

Are you a candidate for the Crown of Life even if your own life doesn't end on a pile of wood, inside a Nazi concentration camp or at the end of a spear?

You betcha. James says this crown is for those who have "stood the test," and that test is whatever trial you are facing. It can be the struggle against temptation (which James immediately writes about in the following verses), staying faithful when you are wronged, or any trial where the temptation is to run or cave in but you stay strong. Most of the saints I am writing about had to do that "unto death," but for the majority of us, that ultimate sacrifice won't be required. What we all have, though, is an opportunity to cling to Jesus in the middle of our current trial, holding on to Him for dear life when there is death all around. An unanswered prayer, a persistent illness, a wayward child, a cold spouse, a fractured relationship, the death of a dream—these are the trials in which we can prove our Crown of Life mettle.

As Matthew Henry noted in his commentary on this section in James:

> To be approved of God is the great aim of a Christian in all his trials; and it will be his blessedness at last, when he shall receive the crown of life. The tried Christian shall be a crowned one: and the crown he shall wear will be a crown of life. It will be life and bliss to him, and will last forever. We only bear the cross for a while, but we shall wear the crown to eternity.[43]

I love that, "The tried Christian shall be a crowned one." Jesus plans to honor you for the way you remained faithful to Him through trials because He has a special place in His heart for overcomers.

The Pioneer and Perfecter

We've walked down the Great Cloud of Witnesses Hall of Fame together, admiring just a few of these suffering saints who endured faithfully until the end. There are many more in the future who will be added to their ranks:

> When he opened the fifth seal, I saw under the altar the souls of those who had been slain because of the word of God and the testimony they had maintained. ¹⁰ They called out in a loud voice, "How long, Sovereign Lord, holy and true, until you judge the inhabitants of the earth and avenge our blood?" Then each of them was given a white robe, and they were told to wait a little longer, until the full number of their fellow servants, their brothers and sisters, were killed just as they had been. (Revelation 6:9-11)

All of these faithful ones receive great honor in heaven, whether that is a Crown of Life or a special white robe.

But the One standing at the end of that hall deserves the highest honor. Jesus is our example, the One who went before and who goes before us. The writer of Hebrews notices the "great crowd of witnesses" in the stands, and then he turns our attention to our Great Champion in the arena.

> And let us run with perseverance the race marked out for us, fixing our eyes on Jesus, the pioneer and perfecter of faith. For the joy set before him he endured the cross, scorning its shame, and sat down at the right hand of the throne of God. Consider him who endured

such opposition from sinners, so that you will not grow weary and lose heart. (Hebrews 12:1-3)

Jesus is our ultimate example, "the pioneer and perfecter of faith," the One who endured unimaginable suffering and remained true to His mission to redeem humanity for the glory of God. He made it to the other side of the shameful cross to a place of joy and honor in heaven.

He invites us to follow Him to the end of our earthly race with stubborn persistence. It's possible to not lose heart on this long race, even when we are struggling through disappointments and encountering opposition. Our Pioneer and Perfecter leads us on. He is the one who makes us "more than conquerors," and, believe it or not, is interceding for us to stand strong:

Christ Jesus who died—more than that, who was raised to life—is at the right hand of God and is also interceding for us. Who shall separate us from the love of Christ? Shall trouble or hardship or persecution or famine or nakedness or danger or sword? As it is written:

"For your sake we face death all day long;
we are considered as sheep to be slaughtered."

No, in all these things we are more than conquerors through him who loved us. For I am convinced that neither death nor life, neither angels nor demons, neither the present nor the future, nor any powers, neither height nor depth, nor anything else in all creation, will be able to separate us from the love of God that is in Christ Jesus our Lord. (Romans 8:34-39)

It's the love of God that is in Christ Jesus our Lord that empowers us for the long haul and makes it all worth it. May we see the twinkle of joy in His eyes in every hard season and especially at the finish line.

Lord, thank You for the testimony of the great cloud of witnesses, both in Your Word and in church history. I am inspired by the testimonies of their lives. In my own life, which seems so much more comfortable by comparison, I want to endure the trials which come my way and remain faithful to You, being thankful in all circumstances. Help me to fix my eyes on You, persevering Savior. You endured the Cross with joy set before You. In whatever trial or opposition I'm facing, help me to more deeply consider the way of the Cross, so that I will not grow weary and lose heart. O Lord, I confess that I grow weary and lose heart so easily, even in such trivial trials. Strengthen me with a clearer vision of You, a stronger value of thankfulness, and orient my life toward Your honor. Thank You that You are interceding for me— that honestly amazes me. I am so grateful that nothing can separate me from Your love. Transform me with that love amid my current challenges and make me more than a conqueror by Your empowering grace. Make me someone who makes You proud. Amen.

CHAPTER SEVEN

THE CROWN OF RIGHTEOUSNESS

---

*"Now there is in store for me the crown of
righteousness, which the Lord, the righteous Judge,
will award to me on that day—and not only to me,
but also to all who have longed for his appearing."*

— 2 Timothy 4:8

Nikolaus Ludwig von Zinzendorf was born in 1700 to a wealthy and privileged family in Germany. Though raised in a Christian stream of pietism, Ludwig adopted the standards of the noble class he grew up with, becoming an entitled count unconcerned by the plight of his poor countrymen who served his estate. But once when he was a teenager and visited an art museum, he saw a painting of the Crucifixion with the inscription, "All this I have done for you. What have you done for me?"

Nikolaus' heart was cut to the quick and he soon gave his life totally to Jesus. His relationship with the Savior grew strong and sweet.

When Nikolaus was 22, a group of Protestant refugees from neighboring Moravia sought shelter from persecution at his estate in Herrnhut, Germany. The count allowed them to move into his large Berthelsdorf estate, and soon after setting up houses and shops, there was much bickering among the stressed-out residents. Nikolaus worked with the group's leader, an itinerant carpenter, to try to settle the quarrels and form a more spiritually healthy community.

The two men led the inhabitants of the new village to cry out to God together in regular prayer meetings. On an August night in 1727, God answered their prayers in a way beyond what any of them could have expected. The Holy Spirit descended that evening in such a beautifully manifest way that their whole community was transformed. Confession of sin flowed. Offended parties repented and were reconciled. A prayer meeting started that evening where shifts of these newly revived Moravian believers would pray around the clock all week long.

Spiritual renewal continued to sweep through the community, but it didn't stop there. This was not a zealous group of Christian mystics who cloistered themselves away from the world—their love for Jesus compelled them outward.

In 1731, Count Zinzendorf met a black man named Anthony Ulrich who had lived as a slave on the island of St. Thomas and had since been freed. Anthony was invited to share his testimony and he pleaded with them to send missionaries to his homeland. Two prominent men volunteered to go to St. Thomas and reach enslaved people with the freedom of the Gospel, one of them willing to sell himself into slavery to have closer access to those he wanted to reach. That sending and sacrifice lit a missions fire in their community.

Even though it was a small community, with only about 300 people at the time, more and more missionaries were sent out. As more Moravian believers left their familiar surroundings for foreign fields, their custom became to wave goodbye on departing boats to teary friends on the shore, shouting out, "The Lamb is worthy to receive the reward of His sufferings!" That phrase became their motto, and they backed it up with action.

The fellowship grew even as more missionaries were sent out to far-flung outposts all over the world: the Caribbean islands, North and South America, the Arctic, Africa and Asia. People were trained in practical skills like shoemaking so that they could live anywhere on the planet.

Their local church-based missions movement in the following two decades sent out more missionaries than all Protestants and Anglicans had sent out in the previous two centuries! The prayer meeting that started during the spiritual renewal continued unabated, 24 hours a day, for 100 years! The prayer room became a furnace that stoked their missions fire and ignited passion in the hearts of the intercessors. Within 150 years, this movement sent out a total of 2,158 of its members to countries all over the world, in the days where there was no electricity, much less computers, cars or airplanes. Nothing stopped them from making Jesus' Name famous to the ends of the earth.

John Wesley, who started the Methodist movement, was converted after his contact with Moravians on a ship crossing the Atlantic. He was struck by how they embraced menial tasks with joy, like volunteering to clean the toilets and swab the decks, chores that Wesley and his fellow Englishmen felt were beneath them. The Moravians' value for humility, passion for Jesus and willingness to pay any price for their beloved Lamb, worthy to receive the reward of His suffering, deeply convicted him and caused him to repent.

Their movement was steeped in a vibrant love for Jesus and overflowed into a passion for His name to be known in all the earth. Their fire lit up thousands of souls just like John Wesley's.

What was the hidden secret of this movement's founder, a man who didn't know at the time he would have such a history-changing impact? Simply put, it was his love and longing for God. It was said that people could hear him whispering prayers under his breath to his "Fairest Lord Jesus."

It wasn't just that Zinzendorf was a brilliant thinker and leader (which he was); it was his love and longing for his heavenly King that lit him up for decades. Zinzendorf actually shied away from diving too deeply into the timetables of eschatology as he considered it a profound biblical mystery that was too sacred to argue about. As one biographer noted on Zinzendorf's end-times theology, "Even more important than the future is the coming of the Savior into the world and his coming to the heart."[44]

For Zinzendorf, the mystery of the Savior coming to the heart was enough to ponder over and marvel about for a lifetime. His favorite phrase was *Umgang mit dem Heiland*, which simply means "living with the Savior." The sweet communion that the humble count had with his Savior brightened his countenance and infused his life with an intangible longing for more of God, greatly impacting everyone he encountered.

During his very busy life he wrote 2,000 hymns—just think of that! Amid the countless meetings, travels, attending to urgent church and property business, the settling of disputes and the endless correspondence of a man of his stature in that day, the count found time to write a couple of thousand hymns! One of them, translated into English by John Wesley, is entitled "I Thirst, Thou Wounded Lamb of God." Part of one of the choruses rings out,

How can it be, Thou heavenly King,
That Thou shouldst us to glory bring;
Make slaves the partners of Thy throne,
Decked with a never-failing crown?[45]

I like to imagine one day in heaven seeing Zinzendorf, though he always considered himself a slave to the Lamb on earth, "decked with never-failing crown" in that glorious realm. He very personally embodied this value of loving and longing for the person of Christ, and that loving and longing lit up a community that lit up the world. Heaven holds a very special crown to honor that longing.

Honoring Longing

There is a special sign of honor in heaven for those longing for the brightness of Christ's glory to be fully revealed, which will ultimately take place at His second coming. Paul wrote to his young disciple Timothy:

Now there is in store for me the crown of righteousness, which the Lord, the righteous Judge, will award to me on that day—and not only to me, but also to all who have longed for his appearing. (2 Timothy 4:8)

The biblical sense for that word "appearing" in Greek, *epipháneia*, means a full manifestation of the advent of Christ—it is both past and future, a bright, fully fledged reveal. *Epipháneia* is where we get our English word "epiphany." Some church traditions celebrate the Epiphany at Christmas, which celebrates the manifestation of Christ to the Gentiles as represented by the Magi in the book of Matthew. In a more modern context, it means an experience of a sudden and striking realization. The researcher had a real epiphany, you might hear, as she was doing her lab work and the answer to a complex problem turned on like a light bulb in her head. Bright, full revelation.

Part of the longing for the *epipháneia* of Christ is that we yearn for the Day when everything is made right. No more injustices! People who got away with vileness get away with it no longer. All unjust suffering ceases on that Day, and the innocent are finally liberated and are now celebrating. Think of the grand finale ending scenes of epic movie franchises like *Star Wars*, *The Lord of the Rings* trilogy or *The Chronicles of Narnia*. The citizens of these realms erupt in celebration in those end scenes because their heroes have vanquished evil. In the heavenly realm, we will be celebrating our champion Jesus for eternity because He has overcome injustice, death and the enemy.

Part of that *epipháne* longing is to live in a perfect place. The designer is the one who thought up pastel sunrises over white sandy beaches. In this pristine perfection there will be no pollution and no more decay. Order and beauty everywhere in a new heaven and a new earth.

Another part of that *epipháne* longing is for our physical bodies to be restored. Our coming resurrection bodies, Paul wrote to the Corinthian believers, will be raised imperishable, in glory and in power (1 Corinthians 15:42-44). And these bodies are something else. No more sickness. No more colds and cancer. No more ailing effects from old age. No more cruel suffering and slipping away on death beds. Unending vitality.

In his well-researched book *Imagine Heaven*, pastor and author John Burke weaves in documented stories of people who have had near-death experiences (NDEs) as he fleshes out the coming perfections of heaven. Burke envisions the astonishing moment of bodily transformation:

Just imagine, that point of life you feared most—the death of your earthly body—suddenly frees you in a way you never anticipated. You feel alive! In fact, so much yourself and so alive that you have to adjust. It takes a little time to realize you're no longer in your earthly body. You still have a body—arms, legs, fingers, and toes—but you begin to realize that something's different as well. It's the same, but different. An upgrade![46]

Perfect justice, breathtaking beauty, and an upgraded body pulsating with vitality...sure sounds good to me! A voice from the throne in John's revelatory vision sums up the new reality this way:

He will wipe every tear from their eyes. There will be no more death or mourning or crying or pain, for the old order of things has passed away. (Revelation 21:4)

Deep down we know we were made for this perfect place where the new order of reality will reign. We feel dissatisfied when the current order of reality disappoints. Justice not served. Scenery ruined by decay. Our bodies languishing in sickness and our loved ones taken away in death.

C.S. Lewis wrote about our relentless disappointment in his made-for-skeptics book *Mere Christianity*: "If I find in myself desires which nothing in this world can satisfy, the only logical explanation is that I was made for another world."[47]

Yes, we were made for another world! We feel the yearning for that perfect, new order. Sometimes we get fleeting glimpses of it on earth when our souls are struck by a revelation of glory and worship, yet those moments feel like a small, teasing appetizer as we wait for that eternal, enriching meal.

The more we align our lives on earth with God's eternal heavenly Kingdom, the more we will yearn for Him in that perfect place. We feel our true north compass pointing away from the flakiness and frustration of this temporal realm and toward the perfection of that eternal one. Paul described the difference between those whose minds are set here and those whose minds are set there:

> Their mind is set on earthly things. But our citizenship is in heaven. And we eagerly await a Savior from there, the Lord Jesus Christ, who, by the power that enables him to bring everything under his control, will transform our lowly bodies so that they will be like his glorious body. (Philippians 3:19b-21)

That phrase "eagerly await" is a strong verb in the Greek, *apekdechomai*, and it carries a sense of yearning and lovesick longing. Paul used this word when he wrote about the creation waiting "in eager expectation for the children of God to be revealed" (Romans 8:19).

Those of us with a citizenship in heaven are severely homesick, even for a place we have never been before. Yet even more than a longing for the Kingdom realm where everything is made right, our deepest longing is the one for the King. What we have experienced of Him in this imperfect realm makes us yearn for the perfect realm where He is fully King, unimpeded, and unhindered and reigning in His fully revealed glory. Even more than a longing for a perfect place, perfect bodies and perfect system, the Crown of Righteousness is for those who yearn for the perfect King.

The Deepest Longing

There is something holy and pure about longing.

As I mentioned before, my wife Stephanie and I were high school sweethearts and then dated through college minus our sophomore year when we broke up and started dating other people. At the end of that year, I came to my senses, realizing that I couldn't let the most wonderful woman in the universe slip away, and so I pursued her again. I was so ecstatic when she gave me a second chance, and at the end of our junior year we got engaged. I wanted us to get married that Christmas break of our senior year, desiring to be together at long last, but our parents thought it wiser if we graduated college first. We set a wedding date for the week after we graduated college, which meant a 13-month engagement.

By the time we started our engagement, we had already been dating for over four years, so all that equaled a long time for longing. The summer right after we got engaged, Stephanie went away on a 10-week mission trip to Guatemala and I couldn't wait to see her face again (these were the days before Facetime of course!). I still remember the moment when I saw her for the first time after that trip. She was walking down a staircase toward the place where we met, looking so stunningly beautiful. My soul radiated with joy to have her back again.

Our long courtship was marked by longing. Part of that was the natural yearning for physical intimacy, for sure. Waiting for our wedding night took a loooongggg time, and we tried hard to live and walk in purity with the help of some people who were discipling us and holding us accountable.

I know waiting for sexual intimacy is hard, but I tell dating and engaged couples now that the yearning to be together physically is one unique season you will never get back again. It's special. You will look back in fondness at the days you were pining for one other. Our culture demands shortcuts and instant satisfaction, but as the verse and the accompanying motto goes, true love waits.

Contrast the regrettable morning after a one-night stand when two people are embarrassed to wake up in the same bed and scramble away from each other as quickly as possible, to the morning after a wedding night when the new bride and groom are delighted to be in each other's arms, knowing that their intimacy will be a guarded gift for each other during their entire lifetimes. The yearning for that moment, as hard as it is, makes the culmination all that more sacred.

On the 100th day of our countdown to our wedding day, Stephanie presented me with a jar of 100 peppermints. There was a note on the jar instructing me to eat one a day before our wedding day...fun idea! But I remember how slowly that pile went down, every morning just taking one little peppermint. I was longing for our wedding day, and in my mind, it couldn't come fast enough. But the days dragged by slowly, and there was a lot of waiting—and a lot of peppermints—between then and my wedding day. I just wanted us to be together, not just for our wedding night, which I was definitely looking forward to, but to no longer be separated. No more saying goodbyes at the end of dates. No more living in different places. Togetherness finally ending all the separation.

The day came where I finally popped in the last peppermint, put on a rented tux and got ready for our wedding day. I was so happy that the long waiting had ended, and I would be with my beautiful bride from this point forward. No more living with stinky college roommates (no offense, stinky college roommates). I was going to live in our new apartment that we had just signed a lease on in a cool city (Austin). But the happiest, most joyful part of this new season was unhindered relationship with my bride.

Yes, we were excited about our wedding day, seeing all our friends and family in one place, all the nuptial traditions. It was for sure a lovely ceremony, but the deepest joy of our hearts was to no longer have to endure separation and to finally be together as one.

That is the truest sense of *apekdechomai* longing. Even stronger than the longing for the Day, there is the longing for a Person, the *epipháneia* of Christ. The best part of heaven, I promise you, is the King of heaven. Taking Him in and seeing Him fully revealed will take your breath away for all eternity. Beholding Him whom your soul has longed for your whole life (whether you were fully conscious of that or not) in unbroken togetherness will satisfy your pining soul at long last. The place is great, don't get me wrong, but what lights it up is the King.

> The city does not need the sun or the moon to shine on it, for the glory of God gives it light, and the Lamb is its lamp. (Revelation 21:23)

It was what Paul was talking about when he wrote to his friend Titus:

> For the grace of God has appeared that offers salvation to all people. It teaches us to say 'No' to ungodliness and worldly passions, and to live self-controlled, upright and godly lives in this present age, while we wait for the blessed hope—the appearing of the glory of our great God and Savior, Jesus Christ... (Titus 2:11-13)

It's not just a longing for the heavenly realm, which is for sure going to be awesome, but it's the bright "appearing of the glory of our great God and Savior, Jesus Christ."

Read that packed phrase again, a little slower this time. "The appearing of the glory of our great God and Savior, Jesus Christ." The appearing of His right-there-in-front-of-you glory will make you wish you had another 1,000 lifetimes to live solely for Him and His glory, yet you will be so satisfied to just finally be together with your great God and Savior. This invisible One you have yearned for your whole life and down to the inmost parts of your soul, fully visible and yours to enjoy forever.

Toward the end of Paul's life, he wrote to his apprentice Timothy from within a prison cell. It would end up being his last recorded epistle, and in it he reflected on finally meeting his Savior Champion face to face:

> For I am already being poured out like a drink offering, and the time for my departure is near. I have fought the good fight, I have finished the race, I have kept the faith. (2 Timothy 4:6-7)

In the very next verse he writes about his confidence of receiving the honor of the Crown of Righteousness, because throughout the long marathon of his life, his deepest yearning was for the manifestation of the Person of Christ:

> Now there is in store for me the crown of righteousness, which the Lord, the righteous Judge, will award to me on that day...

And then he throws out this great little kicker, an invitation to all of us:

> ...and not only to me, but also to all who have longed for his appearing. (2 Timothy 4:8)

This invitation is for you. Yes, you are a candidate for the Crown of Righteousness!

As choked as your life might feel right now with "life's worries, riches and pleasures" (Luke 18:14), all those distractions that crowd out Kingdom life, you still have time to reorient your life to the King. From this point forward, with His grace of course, you can aim your life toward a singular devotion to Christ and a deeper longing for His presence.

"The crown of righteousness is God's reward for a faithful and righteous life," wrote Warren Wiersbe in his Bible commentary, "and our incentive for faithfulness and holiness is in the promise of the Lord's appearing. Because Paul loved His appearing and looked for it, he lived righteously and served cheerfully."[48]

The jewel in the Crown of Righteousness is not just a longing for the end of your long, hard race, but a yearning for the Person who stands at the finish line. Jesus will honor you for the longing that He finds in your heart at the very moment your longing is finally satisfied.

It's amazing that you will get rewarded for the very thing He worked in you, a longing that was stirred by His Spirit. You'll fully realize how He patiently drew you to Himself, revealed His tender love, fashioned you into a worshipper in spirit and truth, and left you wanting more.

Yes, you made some room for Him in your heart and life. But who wouldn't if they saw Him now like this? Your little yes on earth equals dazzling, unimaginable glory in heaven.

You have tasted and seen on earth that He is good, and in that place you will know His fully manifest goodness at long last. The glorious King perfectly revealed in His glorious Kingdom. The brightness and glory from His smile toward you worth infinitely more than the greatest treasures of the world's greatest kingdoms all put together.

Finally together. Forever.

Lord, thank You for holding up this value in your Word of longing for Your appearing. I confess that I am too easily satisfied with worldly pursuits, and I ask that You would bring me to a place of dissatisfaction more quickly for those things that deceive and distract me. Declutter my soul, Lord. Grant to me a truer, more colorful picture of heaven and stir in me a deeper yearning for Your appearing. Capture my imagination, King of Heaven. You and only You satisfy the truest longing of my heart. I know it pleases You when You see that longing in me, so stir it up even more. Make me a worshipper in spirit and truth. May that yearning for You grow in the secret place of my life, so much so that I could be considered a candidate for the Crown of Righteousness. Lord, I eagerly await that great Day when Your glory is fully revealed and I finally see You face to face. Amen.

CHAPTER EIGHT

THE CROWN OF EXULTATION

For who is our hope or joy or crown of exultation? Is it not even you, in the presence of our Lord Jesus at His coming? For you are our glory and joy.

— *1 Thessalonians 2:19-20, NASB*

In my early spiritual formation and throughout the last few decades of following Jesus, I have been deeply inspired by the lives of Floyd and Sally McClung.

In college, when I was wrestling through the big decision and ramifications of making Jesus Lord over every aspect of life, I read Floyd's book, *Living on the Devil's Doorstep*. The autobiography chronicles their decision to leave the U.S. as a young couple and move to Afghanistan to minister to drugged-out hippies along the heroin trail that ran through that country in the '70s. So many great stories of bringing God's hope to very broken people in a very broken place. Then the McClungs spent their next season of life as a young family starting a drug outreach ministry in Amsterdam, right in the middle of the infamous red-light district. I remember reading stories of Floyd and Sally walking their kids to school past places of prostitution and loving and serving the people who lived there so well. They raised their kids literally right on the devil's doorstep. And the thing that impacted me so much was that they seemed to thrive as a family doing it. Their lives were filled with joy even as they poured it out for others.

I thought, *Man, here is a guy who is radically going for it with his family and he seems to be doing okay, seems pretty happy.* It was in the '80s when I read that book so I may have even mentally added... *Totally awesome!*

Around that time, I started to feel a pull toward cross-cultural missions and wondered how that would affect the rest of my life. Would that decision lead me to a life of miserable drudgery, ultimately destroying my future family? The McClungs' book shouted out: *No way!* Floyd and Sally's example inspired me to aim for a life of Kingdom adventure over ease and comfort.

The wording of their book title comes from a famous poem by missionary and evangelist C.T. Studd:

Some want to live within the sound
Of church or chapel bell;
I want to run a rescue shop,
Within a yard of hell.[49]

Floyd and Sally did just that with their family—they ran a rescue shop within a yard of hell, and their lives impacted countless others for eternity.

Over the following years, I heard Floyd speak at our own church and at missions conferences. Every time I did, I came away with that same stirring not to settle for the safety of chapel-bell proximity. As he delivered challenges to a comfortable and entitled-leaning church, he somehow did it with a smile. Floyd is not a sour person at all but has a great sense of humor. Tall guy. Booming voice. Large presence. Yet he laughs often and his stories are sprinkled with lighthearted wit. He's fueled not by an obnoxious type of religious fervor but rather joyful zeal.

Even as his reputation in the church at large grew, he could still laugh often and not take himself too seriously, holding on to the value of learning from anyone. As a young man in my 20s, I was invited with my pastor to go to a Youth With A Mission discipleship training school that Floyd and Sally were leading in southern Colorado. It was such an honor for me to be receiving teaching in person from one of my heroes, someone who had significantly impacted my own life. During the session that my pastor led, I was invited to share with the group about some principles and practicals our church was learning on how to lead multiplying small groups. As I got up to share with the room full of about 40 people, mostly young people that Floyd and Sally were pouring into, Floyd was sitting on the floor and taking copious notes. It was honestly a little unnerving for me...why was this giant of the faith taking notes from a pipsqueak like me? There he was in his 60s, sitting on the floor and learning eagerly from a young man in his 20s who barely knew what he was talking about.

In my 40s when I was going through some transition, having served overseas for about 14 years and then back on staff with our U.S. sending church, Floyd came through town for our church's annual board of advisors' meeting. Our church was going through some transition of its own, and Floyd was there to offer his wise and gentle counsel. I remember sitting next to him at a round table for a dinner with the staff and elders of our church, Floyd listening intently to the discussion as he fiddled with decorations on the table and tore a napkin into dozens of little bits. (I also felt very justified, as in long meetings I too am a fiddler of nearby objects and destroyer of napkins. "See," I told my wife afterwards, "great minds think alike.") I asked Floyd after the meeting if we could get a coffee, and he graciously agreed, even though his schedule in our city had already been packed out fully. We spent over an hour together at a little coffee shop, and I pumped him with questions about transition. I remember him smiling with that delightful twinkle of joy in his eye as he gave me some solid advice, peppered with funny stories.

Just a few months after our coffee shop visit, back in South Africa, Floyd had a medical crisis. At the time of this writing he has not fully recovered from it and is unable to talk very much at all. At this point in his journey, there is no more speaking at conferences and no more face-to-face meetings with those he is discipling. His wisdom, however, lives on in the hundreds of people he has mentored and in the thousands of people (like me) he has inspired through his powerful teachings and potent books.

Sally cares for him so well, even amid her own current health challenges. My wife and I are always moved when we read her updates. Here's a little taste from her recent Facebook post, writing about hope amid the COVID-19 pandemic, Floyd's diminished state and her own health challenges:

I've been asked how to respond to all this. I have to say that I'm learning along with everyone else! I'm not an expert. But there are things I've been learning in recent years that help me in this current time. The most powerful tool I've found to respond to all these challenges is worship and praise. Praise is the way to strength! When our hearts are filled with gratitude, we find that we have more to be grateful for—it opens our eyes.

When I'm anxious - I worship!
When I'm fearful - I worship!
When I feel overwhelmed - I worship!
When I'm sick - I worship!
When I have more questions than answers - I worship!
When I'm tired and weary - I worship!
When I feel like things are out of control - I worship!
When I feel weak - I worship![50]

What wisdom from a godly woman whose life has been refined in the fire over and over and who comes away from those trials with praise and gratitude. I'm so grateful for faithful saints like Floyd and Sally McClung who have persevered and have shared all that refined-in-the-fire gold with us. They have been generous with these priceless treasures, whether in books, on a stage, through social media or in one-on-one meetings. Always heartfelt. And always with us in mind.

In short, their lives are all about others. I remember being in a small group of mission leaders once, and Floyd was so excited to show us a video about walking in a slum in South Africa with one of his ministry partners and how they were finding open-hearted people there and starting to disciple them. At that stage in life, he could have been enjoying the perks of

Christian celebrity status, but his greatest joy was walking in the dirt of the slums and bringing good news to the poor. I could tell from his exuberant storytelling that his joy knew no bounds when one of those people said yes to Jesus.

It's a Kingdom paradox. The more you pour out your lives for others, the more life you get back in return. The happiest people are not those who are focusing on their own conveniences and comforts but those who are making the focus of their lives all about others. Joy is not a limited resource that gets depleted. It's more of a renewable energy source, kind of like exercise. You would think that the more working out you do, the more tired you would be. The opposite is actually true—that discipline adds more energy to your life.

Pride and Joy

Anyone who knows Floyd and Sally McClung even a little bit would say their lives are marked by joy. And their greatest joy is seeing people whom they have influenced make steps toward Jesus and grow toward maturity in Him. I believe this is something that Paul was getting at when he talked about the "crown of exultation," the deep rejoicing he was certain he would experience in the presence of God upon seeing the lives that he had the honor of impacting:

> For who is our hope or joy or crown of exultation? Is it not even you, in the presence of our Lord Jesus at His coming? For you are our glory and joy. (1 Thessalonians 2:19-20, NASB)

The word exultation here is not to be confused with exaltation, which means to raise in rank. Exultation is a feeling of jubilant elation. Some translations use the phrase "crown of rejoicing" in this passage. It's the Greek word *kauchēsis,* which can mean rejoicing, confidence or boasting, depending on the context.

Sometimes that's a negative boasting, as when James taught his hearers not to confidently assert what was going to happen in the future, but instead to add the caveat that all their plans depended on the Lord's will. "All such boasting is evil," he warned them (James 4:16).

Sometimes that exultation is the best kind of confidence, akin to proud parents rejoicing when their children are selected for honor. Even amid their weaknesses, Paul wrote of his fatherly *kauchēsis* in the Corinthian believers:

I have spoken to you with great frankness; I take great pride in you. I am greatly encouraged; in all our troubles my joy knows no bounds. (2 Corinthians 7:4)

Paul was a spiritual parent of sorts for the people he reached with the Gospel, and he was one proud poppa when he saw them grow in maturity. This "crown of exultation," perhaps more of a heavenly experience than an actual object bestowed, would be the apex of rejoicing for him, to finally see them wholly mature in God's presence.

In another letter, this one to the believers in Philippi, he calls his spiritual children his crown:

Therefore, my brothers and sisters, you whom I love and long for, my joy and crown, stand firm in the Lord in this way, dear friends! (Philippians 4:1)

You get the sense from these passages of the spiritual affection Paul felt for them, with love and longing. Paul wasn't just dispensing cognitive discipleship. These were spiritual sons and daughters whom he genuinely carried in his heart, his pride and joy.

No Greater Joy

In the verses from Paul's letters to the Thessalonians and Philippians above, he connects heaven's honor (crown) with joy. I want to dig further down into this *chara* stuff (the Greek word for joy), not only to get the joy, joy, joy, joy down in our hearts, but also to motivate us to go deeper, deeper, deeper, deeper into the discipleship of others.

The Apostle John had a lot of joys in his life. Think of the miracles he witnessed firsthand by the touch of Jesus and all the stunning revelations he received. Yet for him, this was the highest *chara*:

"I have no greater joy than to hear that my children are walking in the truth." (3 John 1:4)

John, like Paul, lived life out of a full heart and had much affection for those he mentored. He felt deeply connected to them, and their spiritual victories were a source of great joy in his life. Think of these apostles as the annoying parents in the front row of the recital who stand up to take pictures of their children and block the view of everyone else behind them. "That's my boy!" they gush. "That's my girl!" And then they want to show those home videos afterwards to people who really aren't that interested.

Joy is gushy like that. It's delight filled with honor.

It's also deeply relational. The greatest joys are always shared. Can you imagine going to Disney World all by yourself? How sad that would be!

Joy is found in heart connection. "Let's celebrate together," the master in the Parable of the Talents said to his faithful servants (Matthew 25:21 and 23, NLT). There is a togetherness quality to *chara*, hard to experience all by your lonesome.

Marcus Warner and Jim Wilder paint a picture of relational joy in their insightful book, *RARE Leadership*:

> Joy is the twinkle in someone's eyes, the smile from deep inside, the gladness that makes lovers run toward each other, the smile of a baby, the feeling of sheer delight that grows stronger as people who love each other lock eyes, what God feels when He makes His face shine over us, and the leap in our hearts when we hear the voice of someone we have been missing for a long time…Joy is the life-giving feeling of mutual care.[51]

The more deeply connected we are to other people, the more joy we will experience, and the more "life-giving feeling of mutual care" will fill our tanks.

Bring that over to discipleship. The more chances you take to pursue people, the deeper you will go with the people who respond. And the more risks you take in spiritual investment—

giving not only encouragement but also "going there" in the harder conversations—the more spiritual victories you will celebrate together with them, so much so that "no greater joy" will mark your life.

Now bring that over to the context of heaven, a perfect place unmarred by sin, shame, disappointments or broken relationships.

This is how Christian philosopher Dallas Willard writes about the relational joy of heaven in his book *Life Without Lack*:

> You see, the greatest thing you and I can imagine is the fellowship of other loving persons, to love and to be loved, to know, to enjoy, to be with, to adventure, to create. That's what has been going on in heaven forever. There is an everlasting, eternal party that we cannot even begin to imagine."[52]

Heaven will be rich with joy, that deep togetherness with cherished friends and family. Willard is right...it will feel like an eternal party. But I believe the greatest joy there will be seeing the people we have impacted with our lives and rejoicing together in God's presence with them. That's how I imagine the Crown of Exultation experience: being fully united with God at last, basking in His pleasure, and richly enjoying the reunion with beloved people whom we had invested in, who felt more like family than just mentees. An ultimate family reunion with great music blasting in the background.

I imagine Floyd and Sally will have a Crown of Exultation experience at the Judgment Seat of Christ. In the presence of Jesus, they will look back on their lives in a flash, remembering their early decisions to follow Him, embarking on an adventure with Him that would take them around the world, raising their children in dozens of homes on four different continents, and seeing in that crowning moment the scores of faces they have shared with, counseled, comforted and sometimes challenged. They will finally know their full impact on the earth, the fruit of mature believers they trained to pursue lives of Kingdom purpose. Together with Jesus, they will thrill in the sight of people from the United States, Afghanistan, Amsterdam and South Africa, and even other nations that they have touched through short-term mission trips, all rejoicing around God's Throne together. So many stories will be shared that came out of their direct and indirect ministry. So many down-the-line testimonies they will hear from the discipleship environments they created. It will feel like it would take an eternity to hear all the stories that came out of their lives, but that's okay...they will have all the time they didn't have in the world.

To quote an old hymn, what a day of rejoicing that will be![53]

And I imagine amid all that joy and honor, they will point back to Jesus and say, "It was all you, Lord!" They will know in the deepest places of their fully renewed minds that any lasting fruit here was because of His work of unmerited grace in their lives.

Even amid that certainty, I imagine Jesus with a knowing smile in that moment. It will be a look that communicates, yes, it was indeed My work of grace in you, and I thank you for how often you freely submitted to it. It will be a smile that lights up eternity and declares the verdict over their lives: "Well done, good and faithful servants."

Can you imagine any greater joy than seeing a smile on the face of Jesus at the Judgment Seat of Christ?

Imagine knowing you have laid down your life in an honorable way before the King of Kings and seeing a twinkle of joy in His eyes because of it. He has thoroughly reviewed your life, and He is now honoring you for all the people you have influenced toward loving Him and giving their lives toward His Kingdom. He has found you faithful in the way you have built His church.

The verdict rings out, "Well done, good and faithful servant." There is great celebration in His presence, and it's not just between you and Him. It's a communal feast of joy with all of you together—Him, you and them—those redeemed lives as a Crown of Exultation.

Yearning for Spiritual Formation in Others

It's good for us to imagine that Day, to motivate us to remember that the most precious things in life aren't things but people! But let's back up from there. What does it look like practically to live your life toward this Crown of Exultation experience?

I think we can go back to the life of the Apostle Paul to see what kind of a lifestyle leads to that kind of fruit and a full assurance of a culmination of joy "in the presence of our Lord Jesus at His coming" (1 Thessalonians 2:19, NASB).

Paul didn't have any physical children, but he had thousands of spiritual children growing up in the dozens of different cities he visited across Asia Minor. He reached out to people in bold evangelism, and the ones who responded he mentored so that they would have a singular devotion to Christ and a depth of spiritual maturity along with godly character.

It was a lot of effort. He likened that yearning for spiritual transformation in his disciples to the painful process of a woman giving birth to a child. To the believers in Galatia, he wrote:

My dear children, for whom I am again in the pains of childbirth until Christ is formed in you... (Galatians 4:19)

That longing was for Christ to be "formed" in them, for them to look so much like Christ in heart and life and conduct that the world would clearly see Jesus in them. He worked toward this end wholeheartedly. Here's how he put it to the believers in Colossae:

He is the one we proclaim, admonishing and teaching everyone with all wisdom, so that we may present everyone fully mature in Christ. To this end I strenuously contend with all the energy Christ so powerfully works in me. (Colossians 1:28-29)

Paul wasn't merely mailing it in. This was no side gig he fiddled with occasionally. Look at the intensity of those words he chose to describe his spiritual mentorship of others: *strenuously, contend, energy, powerfully, works.* These are words charged with intentional action and all based in Christ's passion to see His church grow up into maturity.

You see Paul's longing for their maturity mixed with his fatherly love for them in most of his letters. They are filled with affectionate phrases toward these disciples like, "Night and day we pray most earnestly that we may see you again" (1

Thessalonians 3:10). He cared deeply for these people, and with risk-taking love he oriented his life to helping them to become fully mature in Christ.

In Paul's mind, that final product would be his greatest achievement. In heaven he longed for the Day of collective rejoicing when Christ was finally and fully formed in them. That would be his greatest crown—their transformed lives, now living fully and freely in the presence of the Savior. Exultation throughout eternity.

A Poured-Out Soul

In the late 1800s, a young lady named Lilias Trotter grew up in the privileged upper class of London's West End. In her teens she became interested in art and by her twenties showed a real knack for painting. Once on a trip when she and her mother were staying at a hotel, a prominent art critic of the day happened to be staying there too. Lilias' mother showed this man his daughter's paintings, unbeknownst to her. He was so impressed he invited Lilias into his tutelage with a small group of art students. This mentoring and access to the upper echelons of the art world would surely catapult her into continent-wide fame. Prior to the movie and television revolution, a celebrated artist was about as famous as you could get.

Another of Lilias' passions, as a devout believer, was serving women in London's poorer areas. She volunteered at a YMCA, which at the time was a hostel for poor women holding down menial jobs. She reached out to prostitutes who worked around Victoria Station, offering jobs-skills training which enabled them to escape their debasing trade and find more honorable employment.

In 1887, her life would be forever altered when she heard a message about the millions in North Africa who had never heard the name of Jesus. She began to sense a call to move to Algeria and serve as a missionary there.

This was a pretty radical decision for a single woman living in the Golden Age of Victoria, and it shocked her genteel friends and family. It definitely disappointed the art world. But after some training, off Lilias went, at age 35, to move to Algeria, a place that would be her home for the next four decades. Her love and talent for art never left her, and her journals are filled with sketches and watercolors of the people of Algeria. An observer later wrote about her remarkable work:

> Stamped on every page of her diaries and journals is a woman fully immersed in the practical realities of everyday living even as she is totally engaged in assimilating these realities through an eternal perspective. It is from the tension of these two realities, the seen and the unseen, that hard spiritual truths are hammered out which later appear in her English devotional books and leaflets, elegant and reasoned, and in her Arabic story parables and booklets, sensitively illustrated to satisfy the color-loving Eastern mind and eyes.[54]

I love that picture of her living in the tension of the two realities of the seen and the unseen. Lilias did that well. In her book, *Parables of the Cross,* she wrote about finding one's life by losing it. You definitely don't get the sense that she felt sorry for herself for the choices she had made:

It is the poured-out life that God blesses—the life that heeds not itself, if only other souls may be won. "Ask and it shall be given unto you" is one of God's nursery lessons to His children. "Give, and it shall be given unto you" comes further on. The reason is this: that into the being that is ready to let the self-life go, God the Holy Ghost can come and dwell and work unfettered; and by that indwelling He will manifest within us His wonderful Divine power of communicating vitality—of reproducing the image of Jesus in souls around.[55]

Lilias painted on many canvases in her life, both in her sketchpads and on the lives of Algerians who found Jesus as a result of her poured-out life. That vision of "reproducing the image of Jesus in souls around" sustained her for a lifetime. By the time of her death in 1928, Lilias had established 13 mission stations with over 30 missionaries serving all throughout Algeria, from Arab urban dwellers to Sufi mystics living in the desert. She authored over a dozen books and devotionals that had a huge impact on her generation and are still felt today. They said her methods were a hundred years ahead of her time. I think her secret was that she set her soul on another time, the Day ahead where Jesus would smile and tell the artist, "Well done."

Baby Steps Toward the Crown of Exultation

How about you? Floyd and Sally McClung, The Apostle Paul and Lilias Trotter sound like pretty high standards to shoot for, I know. You may be thinking as I do, swirling about in my own insecurities...will I ever have that Crown of Exultation experience in heaven?

I'm always struck when I think about the audience of Jesus' last words, right before He ascended into heaven. The people hearing these words, which have come to be known as the Great Commission, were a rag-tag group of uneducated villagers. Some of them were struggling with doubt even as Jesus dropped this mind-boggling mandate on them:

> When they saw him, they worshiped him; but some doubted. Then Jesus came to them and said, "All authority in heaven and on earth has been given to me. Therefore go and make disciples of all nations, baptizing them in the name of the Father and of the Son and of the Holy Spirit, and teaching them to obey everything I have commanded you. And surely I am with you always, to the very end of the age." (Matthew 28:17-20)

At this point in the story, these eleven guys were just feeling lucky not to be caught by Roman soldiers and thrown into prison, and here Jesus was telling them to advance into all the known nations of the world. And not only that, but once they got to those nations, they were to disciple the various people groups living there, teaching them to obey everything Jesus had commanded during their three years together. That is one tall order for a group of dumbstruck dudes who could all fit in one small fishing boat together.

Yet those were their marching orders. I'm sure they were thinking, *Who, us?* And I believe that's why Jesus added the kicker, which often gets overlooked when we trip over the massiveness of this passage:

...I am with you always...

Yes, He is with us! He doesn't just send us out from a stationary place and wish us luck on our way, but He walks with us in this mandate! The fuel on that journey is His love and compassion: "Christ's love compels us" (2 Corinthians 5:14). The power on that journey is His Spirit. That's why when He gave His disciples these marching orders, He instructed them first to sit tight in Jerusalem. "I am going to send you what my Father has promised," He told them, "but stay in the city until you have been clothed with power from on high" (Luke 24:49).

You may know the story. Ten days later, the Holy Spirit descended and all heaven broke loose.

From that point in time when those first simple disciples were set ablaze to light up their world all the way down the generations to us who are still advancing that worldwide movement, the secret remains the same. He is with us always.

For from Him, and through Him, and to Him are all things. (Romans 11:36a, NASB)

That's very good news for us! This awesome Great Commission responsibility isn't ours to do on our own and then come report back to Him afterwards. It really is all from Him and through Him and then back to Him, a bedrock truth from the verse above. We walk with Him at the pace of His grace, even while we are on mission. It's not so much for Him but with Him.

This is not a book on how to disciple others, so I'm not going to pull out every tool from the discipler's toolbox. I do however want to leave you with one encouragement to at least take the first step on this long journey. With this culminating Day of heaven's joy in mind, ask God to give you His heart for people. Open your heart to His heart because He so deeply cares for people, and that clean-burning fuel will fire your engine for a long time. The Apostle John got this. This "disciple whom Jesus loved," a title that shows up six times in his Gospel account, later wrote this simple formula toward the end of his life: "We love because He first loved us" (1 John 4:19).

I like the definition of discipleship that my dear friend and mentor Mark Buckner came up with: "Having spiritual ambition for someone else." Mark had a huge impact on me from my college years on, and I love the simplicity of that statement. It's a value that he has lived out decade after decade, not only looking out for his own spiritual growth but having ambition to help others along the way. It's impacted people all over the world, and I'm confident in heaven there is a Crown of Exultation experience coming his way.

Start there. *Lord, give me spiritual ambition for someone else.* I've seen illiterate Javanese farmers in Indonesia, only one week old in the Lord, begin to disciple other people with the elementary truths they had just learned the week before. You don't need years of training for this. Just ask God for His heart for others, then take what He has invested in you and begin to invest it into them. That little investment will grow like a promising mustard plant just as Jesus said it would, eventually becoming the largest tree in the garden (Matthew 13:31-32). It's a sight to behold on earth.

In heaven you will fully behold it, with its intertwining branches and other trees that were born out of its generational growth that wound down through the ages. The stories will be thrilling and nearly endless. So many diverse people with so much joy in their fully renewed faces, celebrating around the Throne, all somehow impacted from a tiny shoot that grew out of a lone seed that you had planted back in the day. Now in this Day, you see the whole picture. You had no idea then and can hardly believe it now, but you are here and so you can. And for you, the best part of this celebratory and crowning moment is the bright smile on Jesus' face.

Lord, thank You for Your heart for me and for the people that You have sent into my life to show me Your love. Thank You so much for their investment in me. I don't want to stop there, Lord, and only focus on Your blessings in my life, which are so many. Show me the people I can invest in, even if it's in a very small way. Give me spiritual ambition for others today. Bring to my mind specific names and faces. I want to grow in Your desire to see them transformed in Your presence, and to see You fully formed in them. Walk with me in this, Lord. Empower me with Your Spirit and fuel me with Your love and compassion toward them. I desire in heaven to have the joyful experience of seeing people who were impacted by Your love through me. Make me a candidate by Your grace for the Crown of Exultation. May my poured-out life bring a smile to Your face on that Day, Lord Jesus!

CHAPTER NINE

STRUGGLE MEETS HEAVEN

When I was 22 and newly married, I worked as an essay grader for a standardized test that the State of Texas inflicted upon fourth graders. My job was to evaluate, on a scale from one to five, how well 10-year-old students could describe a picture of an old-time country store. On the delightfully named State of Texas Assessments of Academic Readiness (STAAR) test day, these kids were given a picture of an old-time country store and then instructed to write descriptively about it using a number two pencil. I evaluated at least 200 essays per shift along with about 100 other people, who, like me, were desperate to find better jobs. Or at least more interesting ones. The essays blurred together *en masse*. After the first week I started keeping count on a little scratch pad of how many times the kids' essays would start with, "Have you ever wondered what an old-time country store looks like?" I very quickly stopped wondering.

The gig was temporary, and the pay wasn't great, but it was enough to put food on the table, which for us at the time was a scratched-up end table we used as we sat on the floor and ate our meals together. Those were the good ol' romantically poor honeymoon nest days. I loved coming home every night but dreaded going to work every day.

The work was grueling, and I felt very little vision for it. Toward the end of the contract, I realized that I was missing an opportunity to reach out to fellow essay graders on breaks and felt the Lord nudging in me that direction. I found another believer who worked there, and we started a Bible study during lunch breaks and invited other people to come to it. No one took us up on the offer so it ended up just being the two of us, but at least we gave it a shot, plus I got some solid Christian fellowship in the middle of super-boring days.

After every last old-time country store essay had been graded, my contract ended and I started the job search again. Those were the days when you had to "pound the pavement"— look for jobs in the newspaper, mail your actual resume and cover letter in the actual mail, call businesses on the actual landline phone, get the runaround by savvy secretaries, apply for posted jobs in person, and sometimes show up at prospective employers' doors unscheduled in an effort to get their attention. Pavement was pounded and so were hearts.

Even as I looked for a new job, I vowed that when I found one I would show up on day one with greater vision, orienting my workday to Jesus.

After much searching, I finally landed a job as a reporter for a new political magazine in Austin called *Politics Today*. The founder and editor was an Asian-American grad student at University of Texas who was studying science but whose real passion was politics. He saved up enough money for his start-up magazine, which he intended to pit against *Newsweek* and *Time*. I was all for that grand dream as long as I got paid.

His limited budget allowed for one full-time reporter and a one-room office in a seedy area of town. I worked eight-hour days and made a lot of phone calls to get interviews (these were the days before the internet made research much easier). No one had ever heard of *Politics Today*, of course, so I had to bluff my way through to get as many interviews as I could. I did long pieces on issues I didn't really understand that well and that very few people would ever read. My new boss, who only came into the office once a week, mostly complained that my work wasn't in-depth enough. I felt it unfair for him to have all these expectations of me while offering no real resources. He hardly ever said a kind word to me. I did enjoy the creative part of the job (it was better than old-time country stores), but as an extrovert, I hated working in an empty office all day by myself.

This passage from Colossians kept my heart alive during those mind-numbing days, and I meditated on it often. It was Paul's advice to the pitiful people who found themselves under an unfair yoke of tyranny:

> Slaves, obey your earthly masters in everything; and do it, not only when their eye is on you and to curry their favor, but with sincerity of heart and reverence for the Lord. Whatever you do, work at it with all your heart, as working for the Lord, not for human masters, since you know that you will receive an inheritance from the Lord as a reward. It is the Lord Christ you are serving. (Colossians 3:22-24)

I kept this passage in the top drawer of my desk and pulled it out often to read it, eventually memorizing and personalizing it: *I am working not for this unfair editor but for the Lord. I will receive an inheritance from the Lord as a reward for being faithful here, so I will do this job with all my heart. It is the Lord Christ whom I am serving.*

I didn't have to wait until the afterlife to get a reward from the Lord. *Politics Today* folded after just two issues and it wasn't long before I found a much better job, one with a dynamic team of people and exciting new challenges. I loved it and worked there for years.

My true boss was never the State of Texas or an unfair grad student. It was and it is the Lord, and He is a rewarder of faithfulness. The one who is faithful in little will be ruler of much—so goes the spiritual principle. But even beyond that, knowing that you are pleasing the Lord even from a place of obscurity brings a sense of hidden joy to your heart.

In whatever place of drudgery or unfairness you find yourself toiling today, know that God is watching you. He is not only watching over you for your good, but also for your coming reward. Sincerity of heart comes out of reverence for Him. You will receive a reward directly from His generous hand. He will promote you and loves to honor faithfulness in the little.

Keeping an eye on heaven literally changes everything. A moment meditating on how God feels about you turns the grind into grace. Just remembering that God is with you and that He will honor you for how your life has pleased Him is like holding up a prism to the light, reflecting back bright patches of color on every surface.

Here are a few more common life struggles, and what it would look like to overlay them with heaven's gaze over your life.

Insecurity

You walk into a room and nervously scan it, wondering who is going to talk to you here. You don't really know the people here that well and there is definitely no one you have been wanting to see. *Why am I even here?* If you are going to get into a conversation, it will be you initiating it. You wish you could swim in the deep end of the pool of meaningful relationships, but you have to start at the shallow chit-chat end, something you're not very good at. The problem is you just don't have enough emotional energy to swim from that end of the pool to the deeper side. You wish you were somewhere else. Wallflower it's going to be tonight.

Other people are talking, looking like they are having an enjoyable time. You just wish you were home in front of your TV or fiddling with your smartphone on your comfy sofa. Why did you even come?

Insecurity Meets Heaven

You walk into a room and nervously scan it, wondering who is going to talk to you here. You don't feel like being here, for sure, and whisper a prayer under your breath. *Lord, give me Your eyes to see in this moment. I don't feel like being here, but I know that You are with me. Give me Your heart for these people and show me if You want me to talk to someone.* You think Jesus just might be hiding in this very room, as this morning you meditated on the story of the sheep and the goats in Matthew 25 where Jesus affirms the caring for the left-out and broken. "Whatever you did for one of the least of these brothers and sisters of mine," you remember reading, "you did for me."

You scan the room again and see someone you recognize standing against the back wall, Styrofoam cup of coffee in hand, looking down and studying the designs on the carpet. You feel a tug to go up and initiate conversation, and you know it must be from heaven because it's definitely not coming from your own heart. You say another silent prayer and walk over. "Hey, I think we have met before, but I forgot your name," you say, mustering your friendliest smile. A startled look, a reciprocated smile, and you start into a conversation that grows deeper and more meaningful. You start to feel heaven's compassion for this person. Later you drive home thanking God for using you to speak some of His truth and show some of His love.

Lust

You are feeling the pull again. It's been a long day, and you want to relax and look at some pictures of pretty girls, just for a few minutes. It won't go anywhere dark, only a few attractive ladies for just a few stolen moments of enjoyment. Even though you have some accountability in your life and a filtering program installed on your computer and phone, you are smart enough to know a way around those electronic fences, and you can always give some vague partial confession later to your accountability partners. Off you go to fantasy land, just for a few minutes...

...After two hours go by, you are drinking in hardcore porn and hating yourself for it, but it's so hard to pull away. *Don't worry about it,* a voice inside you says. *It's too late now and no one will ever know. Plus it's not really hurting anyone.* You agree with the sinister whisper as you keep scrolling through and you think you might as well keep watching, keep enjoying, because you've already blown it. The next morning you feel a hangover of guilt that takes you all day to shake off. You are sore from kicking yourself, feeling the shame of supporting an industry you despise, marred in the way you are relating to real people, and very aware that your addiction is damaging all of your most important relationships.

Lust Meets Heaven

You are feeling the pull again. It's been a long day and you want to relax. As you have been battling the temptation of going toward sexual fantasy for stress relief, you've been meditating on Hebrews 4:13. You pull up the verse from a notepad app on your phone and read it over again: "Nothing in all creation is hidden from God's sight. Everything is uncovered and laid bare before the eyes of him to whom we must give account." You've used this very device before to look at pornography, and now you are using it to look at the perfect law that brings freedom.

You think of the staggering reality of that verse, that this moment matters. God's gaze is on you in this very moment, and you will give an account for how you have lived your life. You realize you can't afford to give yourself over to this temptation, not only because of this moment but because of how you will feel tomorrow and the people it will hurt. Those victims include not only your family, but also the women who are being exploited, your clicks funding their captivity and degradation. *This moment matters,* you say out loud. *Thank You, Lord, that everything in my life is uncovered before You and that one Day I will give an account for how I spend my time. I confess that I need You to break the grip of pornography. Make me a man that can be trusted when no one is looking, and one that helps set others free.* You text a friend and tell him you are feeling the pull and ask him to pray for you. You spend some time praying for the guys you know who struggle with this. This heartfelt intercession turns into a time of worship. You finally drift off to sleep and the next morning feel rested and refreshed, ready for a new day.

Envy

You got passed over for a second promotion. It feels so unfair with how hard you have been working recently. Your colleague, who is better at playing office politics than you, yet works only half as hard, landed it easily with sheer charm. That's the way you read it. After the official announcement you congratulate him along with everyone else. You wonder if under their smiles and congrats they are feeling the same amount of envy as you. What did your boss see in him that she doesn't see in you? Does your hard work go unseen? It certainly feels like it doesn't pay off, and you start wondering if you should start looking for a new place where people see and really appreciate you. You know it's going to be a hard season seeing him rise while you stay in the same spot, grinding it out in the same old cubicle.

Envy Meets Heaven

You got passed over for a second promotion. It feels so unfair, with how hard you have worked recently. Your mantra this season has been "faithful in little," and it's a stinging disappointment that all those little acts of faithfulness have not added up to bigger reward. As you extend a hand of congratulations along with everyone else, you know it is going to be hard for you to see him continue to rise in his career. But you determine inwardly that you are going to be bigger than that. You imagine yourself at the Judgment Seat of Christ, the bright smile of Jesus on you for a life of faithfulness. You tell yourself that character is who you are when no one is looking...and that He is always looking. *No one may ever recognize me on this earth, Lord, but I want my life to be pleasing to You. That's enough for me.* As you think more on this, and imagine that Day, you feel a nudge from the Holy Spirt that you should start praying for your newly promoted co-worker. He is going to need the extra prayer support and you sense that it would even please the Father if you could rejoice with those who rejoice. As you connect with God in prayer, you still feel a sting of disappointment, but you also feel a sense that His eye is on you and that His reward is the one that matters. You're going to keep being faithful in little and trust Him for the outcomes. Even if no one recognizes your hard work on earth and rewards it, you feel an inner joy that His smile on the Last Day is enough.

Hopelessness

Why am I even on this earth? You have been struggling lately just to get out of bed in the mornings, with nothing in your life that you are looking forward to. Nothing. You have a job, which you guess you should be grateful for, but it feels like such a grind. Other people there seem to have a spark, some pep in life, with experiences they are looking forward to, like the weekends and hobbies they give themselves to in their free time. You are on the other end of that spectrum with a stubborn listlessness, struggling with a pervading sense of hopelessness. The only thing you look forward to about this weekend is time to sleep in more. But today is a weekday and you must soldier on. You will yourself to move your legs so that your feet will hit the floor, shuffle slowly toward the bathroom to get ready, while everything in you wants to go back to that warm bed, throw the covers back over your head, and escape to some other far away world. A world where you are at least a little bit happy, even if it's a made-up one. You're tired of feeling down so much. It's quite embarrassing that you can't just shake it off, and you wonder when you are going to turn the page to a new chapter.

God, what's wrong with me? Why can't I just be happy? It seems so effortless for other people and that feels so unfair.

Hopelessness Meets Heaven

Why am I even on this earth? You have been struggling to get out of bed, and that's the familiar first thought that hits you upon waking after a fitful sleep. You're not sure why you have felt so down lately, whether it is neurological or something deeper down, something unconscious from your past. Whatever the case, you have been asking God to bring you hope. You have felt worthless lately and you know somehow only the Worthy One can get you through this. You've made a commitment that every morning, instead of reaching for your phone and scrolling through social media (something that usually makes you feel worse, gazing at people who seem happier than you), you are going to pull that same phone out and open up a Bible app. Today's passage is from John 12, when Jesus predicts his death. One verse pops out, when Jesus said, "Now my soul is troubled" (John 12:27). You whisper a prayer of thanks that Jesus knows what it is to have a troubled soul. *God, I am going through only a small fraction of what You went through, but I thank You that You understand what it's like to have a troubled soul.* You read on, seeing how Jesus chose the harder road of glory for the name of His Father rather than escape from the Cross, something He had every right to request. That's amazing enough. But the next part really strikes you:

> Then a voice came from heaven, "I have glorified it, and will glorify it again."

The crowd that was there and heard it said it had thundered; others said an angel had spoken to him.

Jesus said, "This voice was for your benefit, not mine..." (John 12:28-30)

You are struck with how Jesus was so settled in His identity and certain of His mission. When a voice came from heaven affirming both, He didn't really need it and it seemed to be more of an exclamation point, something extra for His followers. Jesus' identity was attacked over and over, you remember, but somehow the voice of His loving Father was even stronger within Him.

You know that this biblical insight isn't a magic bullet that will vanquish all your depression, and you are grateful for professional help and medication, but you do at least feel a glimmer of hope, that it's possible for your beat-up identity to be repaired and restored by what the Father says about you. That little glimmer is something special to you, as you haven't felt any measure of hope in a while.

You get out of bed and shuffle towards the bathroom to get ready for the day, asking God to give you greater discernment to distinguish His voice from your own condemning one and the lies of the enemy. *God, I don't know what's wrong with me, but I believe that Your truth can get me through it and I choose to cling to You today.*

Comparison

You seem constantly to have your radar up, scanning a room and figuring out who is the fairest maiden of them all. It's definitely not you and you know that. You desperately want to be prettier, thinner, more attractive all around, but somehow your genes, habits and body have not cooperated. You resign yourself to doing the best with what you have, wishing it were more. But today you have to put your beauty game face on as you are attending a wedding, of all things. Great, another reminder of how you are walking life's journey without a life partner. You're happy for the bride and groom, a couple you genuinely care about, but you worry you'll feel an ache of loneliness through the celebration. You can imagine yourself watching the bride gracefully walk down the aisle, feeling more ire in your heart than happiness. *Why can't I be happy? Why does it always evade me? Where is my special someone?*

Comparison Meets Heaven

You seem constantly to have your radar up, scanning a room and figuring out who is the fairest maiden of them all. You've been asking God to deliver you from comparison, something you have struggled with your whole life, and you know today is going to be a tough one. It's a wedding of two good friends, and you imagine that all the accompanying happiness will also pound your self-esteem. This morning you have been reading passages about Jesus the Bridegroom's love for His Bride, anything you could find in the Bible when you googled "Wedding Feast of the Lamb" or the "Bride of Christ." As you journal and meditate on a few sections, you feel a resolve to imagine Jesus at the wedding and His delight in you. You imagine His smile at the Judgment Seat of Christ, welcoming you warmly into heaven. You imagine

His initiating and undying love for His Bride. You think about the moment when your friend walks down the aisle today toward the groom, and you know it's going to send holy shivers down your soul. What a beautiful picture of the Bride being made ready for an adoring Groom. *Thank You, Lord, that I am your beloved and You are mine. If no one seems to pay attention to me, if no one asks me to dance, I know that You still see me and that You delight in me. Give me a greater glimpse of heaven today.* As you ready yourself for the occasion, you feel an anticipation of experiencing some joy in the celebration.

But Wait, There's More...

Those are just a few categories of commonplace struggles. Honestly I can't think of a stubborn life issue that wouldn't be transformed by living in the light of an eternal perspective. You can bring every single struggle fully before the One who sees you and who will reward you for overcoming. You may have a different issue than these examples. Whatever it is, can I recommend you give it a healthy dose of eternity, filtering it through the gaze of the One who sees you, loves you and desires to reward you?

———————

Lord, I confess that I have not been living in the light of eternity. Far from it. I grind through my days with no sense of purpose and I want that to change. I keep cycling through the same sins and addictions and keep falling, over and over. I see how the fleeting pleasures and vanities of this life have marred my soul. O Lord, I want my life to be more about running with

You on the mountains than climbing out of the ditches again and again. I give my struggle to You, here and now. Deliver me from these endless cycles. Envision me for that Great Day when I stand before You. I desire to see a bright smile on Your radiant face at the Judgment Seat of Christ and to know that my life has pleased You. O Lord, I long to honor You every day until then and in every way with the limited time I have on earth. Reorient me toward Your Kingdom. May Your pleasure, my King, be my highest pursuit. Set my heart free with Your smiling gaze over my life today. Amen.

CHAPTER TEN

REDISCOVERING HEAVEN

The first plane flight I can remember happened for me at age 10, a nonstop from Memphis to Tampa. My dad was in Florida for a business conference, and my 13-year-old sister and I got to fly out to meet him for a couple of fun days on the tail end of his trip. My mom checked us in, a flight attendant accompanied us through the journey, and the whole trip for me felt like a thrilling grownup adventure.

As the younger sibling, I got the window seat and I felt mesmerized watching the canopy of clouds float by. I had never seen the billowy white wonders from a high vantage point like that, and I remember thinking how cool it would be to jump up and down on those fluffy clouds like an other-worldly trampoline.

Have you ever had the same thought while you were flying...how fun it would be to jump up and down in a sky bouncy house?

I think for most of us, if those clouds could hold us up and we could somehow breathe while doing it, that would be a whole lot of atmospheric fun. Imagine jumping up and down in a beautiful place and enjoying the sunset on a billowy horizon. Magical.

Would it be fun for 10 minutes?

Sure.

How about an hour?

Maybe for an hour it would still be fun.

How about a whole day? A week?

Now that feels like a stretch. That might get a little boring.

What if I threw in the bonus that there will be angels flying around while you are doing it? How about a month doing that?

Hmm. Maybe after a month, even with accompanying angels, I would get a little tired of doing even that.

How about a year? A decade? A century? A millennium? And remember the whole time you get to float around and fly with angels.

I dunno. Ten thousand years doing something even that cool feels too long. Maybe a day or two, but no longer than that.

If we are being honest, most of us imagine heaven kind of like that, exciting and wonderful at first and then maybe bland the remainder of eternity. A nice place, for sure, but maybe kind of boring long term? God is there and that's cool, but there's no real action, nothing to get excited about. Sort of like *The Far Side* cartoon by Gary Larson where there is a lone guy sitting on a cloud in heaven by himself, with a speech balloon above his head revealing his thoughts: "…Wish I'd brought a magazine."[56]

If we think of heaven as a place where disembodied souls waft around on wispy clouds, then yes, you would definitely want to bring a magazine. John Eldredge articulates this common misconception of heaven in his insightful book, *The Journey* of *Desire*:

> We have made nothing of eternity. If I told you that your
> income would triple next year, and that European

vacation you've wanted is just around the corner, you'd be excited, hopeful. The future would look promising. It seems possible, *desirable*. But our ideas of heaven, while possible, aren't all that desirable...Nearly every Christian I have spoken with has some idea that eternity is an unending church service. After all, the Bible says that the saints 'worship God in heaven,' and without giving it much more thought we have settled on an image of the never-ending sing-along in the sky, one great hymn after another, forever and ever, amen.

And our heart sinks. *Forever and ever? That's it? That's the good news?* And then we sigh and feel guilty that we are not more 'spiritual.' We lose heart, and we turn once more to the present to find what life we can. Eternity ends up having no bearing on our search for life whatsoever. It feels like the end of the search. And since we're not all that sure about what comes after, we search hard now. Remember, we can only hope for what we desire. How can the church service that never ends be more desirable than the richest experience of life here? [57]

Eldredge is trying to challenge our assumptions about heaven so that we will imagine it more correctly and actually desire the place. (He wrote a whole other book on the subject entitled *All Things New*, which I also recommend.) If we believe that heaven is as exciting as listening to hymns for 10,000 years, then for sure most of us are not going to desire it (even if they only sing the first, second and fourth verse of each hymn like I did growing up in a Baptist church). At best, we may imagine heaven in times of grief as the sweet afterlife, a nice place for loved ones to finally Rest in Peace in the Sweet By and By, with soft organ music playing in the background. But still no action there, nothing to get excited about in the regular rhythms of our day-to-day lives.

In his brilliant and challenging book, *Surprised by Hope*, N.T. Wright argues how our Greek-inspired views color our understanding of heaven and give us blind spots when we read biblical passages that spell it out clearly. Words for us like "soul" and "the Kingdom of God" carry with them deeply rooted stereotypes more aligned with Plato's vision of disembodied souls entering bliss than the biblical picture of eternity.

Take for example the word "resurrection." We know from the Gospel accounts that after Jesus died on the Cross, He was resurrected and appeared to His disciples in bodily form, inviting Thomas to inspect his scars (John 20:27), and even eating a fish to prove his point (Luke 24:43). Yet when we think of our own resurrection, we default to Greek-inspired assumptions and imagine the disembodied-souls-floating-around-on-clouds stuff, not actual resurrected bodies ruling and reigning with Christ in a new creation (as in Revelation 5:10). Here's a little taste of Wright's challenge:

> Heaven, in the Bible, is not a future destiny but the other, hidden, dimension of our ordinary life—God's dimension, if you like. God made heaven and earth; at the last he will remake both and join them together forever. And when we come to the picture of the actual end in Revelation 21–22, we find not ransomed souls making their way to a disembodied heaven but rather

the new Jerusalem coming down from heaven to earth, uniting the two in a lasting embrace.[58]

It takes Wright several chapters to pull us out of our Greek-rooted assumptions about heaven. But let me ask you as a little appetizer: what does it do for your anticipation of heaven to imagine yourself having a super body and ruling and reigning with Christ in a colorful new creation, as opposed to wearing a toga and sitting on a fluffy cloud, peacefully strumming a harp? I personally can get fired up more for Wright's biblically richer vision of heaven, where "the redeemed people of God in the new world will be the agents of his love going out in new ways, to accomplish new creative tasks, to celebrate and extend the glory of his love."[59]

That is so intriguing to me, thinking of the ruling and reigning dimension of heaven, teased out in the scriptures (like 2 Timothy 3:12 and Revelation 5:10), but not fully explained. We are left to our imaginations, and for now that will have to do. Dallas Willard, in his theologically rich book, *The Divine Conspiracy*, takes a crack at it when he writes about the Parable of the Talents in Matthew Chapter 25. He muses on what "enter into the joy of your master" might look like:

That "joy" is, of course, the creation and care of what is good, in all its dimensions. A place in God's creative order has been reserved for each one of us from before the beginnings of cosmic existence. His plan is for us to develop, as apprentices to Jesus, to the point where we can take our place in the ongoing creativity of the universe.[60]

In whatever way it turns out, that "ongoing creativity of the universe" is going to be so much more exciting than the bland alternative, propagated in funeral home-vibe assumptions and popular culture stereotypes. I recently watched the Pixar movie, *Soul,* with my family. It's a delightful film about a New York Jazz musician named Joe who never really went for his dreams and falls down a manhole one day, ending his life prematurely. He then gets transported to a weigh station of sorts between earth and the afterlife, and desperately tries all sorts of tricks to get back to earth for another shot at life. I can't blame him for wanting to get back. The way the film depicts the afterlife is an escalator traveling upwards toward a bright light with disembodied souls riding on it, all ready to peacefully merge into radiant nothingness as low hum ethereal music plays in the background. Peaceful for sure, but oh so boring. Cute movie. Terrible theology.

To help us move past these stale stereotypes and gun our engines for heaven, Eldredge encourages us to pay attention to when our hearts are deeply moved by something on earth. He argues that when we are touched by experiences or storylines, our hearts may be casting a signal toward heaven. As he expressed it in a podcast, "There is a heart that God put within you, and every story that you love, everything that stirs you to passion is reminding you of the life that you were meant to live, that you were created to live."[61]

The life we were created to live is fully realized in heaven, the place where God's Kingdom has fully come at last. It's the great culmination of all things being reconciled and restored, not ethereal and bland nothingness.

I want my kids to understand heaven as something mind-blowing and to develop a longing for it, to see it as the colorful and exciting place it is and not the fluffy, cloudy, boring-waiting room kind of place. I've often used this analogy with them, especially when they were younger and could think of no better place on earth to go than Disney World. My in-laws live in Orlando and used to work at Disney, so we have gotten to go many times during our home assignments with their golden-ticket guest passes.

I say something like, "Hey, did you know that there is a Disney World in heaven?"

"Really?"

"Yep. You can go anytime you want, as many days as you want, and it's totally free. Open 24 hours a day...go any time you like."

"Wow!" one of them says while the older ones roll their eyes because they know what theological point is coming.

"Yeah, it's true. But it's always empty."

"Huh? What? Why?"

"Well, it's so boring.

"No way! Disney World could never be boring."

"Well heaven is so exciting, why would anyone ever want to go to that boring place called Disney World? You could go there, but why in heaven would you want to?"

"No way."

"Yes, totally empty. The other stuff in heaven is just too exciting. But if you really want to go, you still can."

Hopefully some good theology is soaking into their brains behind their shocked expressions.

I realize this may not seem like a scripturally solid metaphor, but I figure that if God can do "abundantly beyond what we ask or imagine" (Ephesians 3:20), surely the furthest stretch of my limited imagination is the weakest painting of heaven ever. King Solomon, in his profound book of philosophy and wisdom, declared that God has "set eternity in the human heart" (Ecclesiastes 3:11). There is a deep-calling-to-deep yearning for eternity in our hearts, and I believe it's okay to try to actively stir our imagination toward heaven so that we will truly desire the place.

Richard Foster, in his classic book, *Celebration of Discipline*, argues for using the faculty of our God-given imagination to root us more richly into God-given truths:

> But just as we can believe that God can take our reason (fallen as it is) and sanctify and use it for his good purposes, so we believe he can sanctify the imagination and use *it* for his good purposes...God created us with an imagination, and as Lord of his creation he can and does redeem it and use it for the work of the Kingdom of God.[62]

When it comes to heaven, our imagination is an ally to help stir us toward eternity. John Burke puts it this way in *Imagine Heaven*:

> Heaven sounds like a place of imaginative fictional fantasy. But maybe the reason we possess within us such imaginative fictional capacity is because of a longing for eternity that God placed in the human heart. Like a bird's homing instinct, it's pointing us homeward.[63]

In this final chapter I want us to tune in to that homing instinct. Let's assume Foster's take on imagination is true, frame heaven more biblically as N.T. Wright does, and then take up Eldredge on his challenge, paying attention to when our hearts have been deeply moved by something downright heavenly. This is an attempt to help us get heaven a little more right, to paint it in our imaginations as a place so amazing that even Disney World (or whatever dopamine-hit experience on earth you would most desire) would really seem boring by comparison. I hope you will indulge my imagination as we think about four elements of heaven, each so extremely pleasurable that you will need that brand-new resurrection body just to handle it: colorful celebration, flawless perfection, longed-for consummation, and staggering honor.

Colorful Celebration

I'm a sucker for the opening ceremonies of the Olympics. I almost always find a way to watch them live, no matter if I am in the U.S. or overseas, and no matter the difference in time zones.

I can't help myself. There is something so moving about the whole world tuning in to this bright festival of the nations, right on the cusp of a global competition between the very best athletes of those nations representing their countries with patriotic pride.

First comes the "artistic program," which welcomes the Olympics with a cultural flourish of the host country. I remember watching the 2012 Summer Olympics in London, which for me was at 2 a.m. local time in Indonesia (and which I paid for the next day). But it was worth every yawn that following day.

The whole jaw-dropping spectacle was called "Isles of Wonder" and was directed by the Academy Award-winning British director Danny Boyle (who also directed *Slumdog Millionaire*). A total of 60,000 people were in attendance, including Queen Elizabeth II who opened the ceremony. Eighty heads of state. A performance by Paul McCartney. Dancing. Lights. Shakespeare. History. Celebration. You get the grand picture.

And I remember the opening ceremony of the 2018 Winter Olympics in PyeongChang, South Korea. Mercifully this one was broadcast during my normal waking hours, but the cultural wonder of that program would have definitely been worth a poor night's sleep. Five kids dressed in parkas and wearing colors of the five Olympic rings walked in on top of a circular video disk with a Korean mythological white creature, making it look like they were exploring in the snow. What happened next would be nearly impossible to describe (look it up on YouTube). The bland title of "artistic program" does no justice for this cultural panoramic feast.

No amount of time or expense is spared to put on these showcases. The performers of the PyeongChang opening ceremony had practiced since October of the previous year to put on their cultural showcase—over half a year! For the 2008 Winter Olympics in Beijing, an estimated $100 million dollars was spent! Stadiums are built years ahead of time just to get ready. The whole world is watching and the whole world is rarely disappointed.

Next comes the "parade of nations." I love watching the athletes stream into the stadium, carrying their flags to represent their beloved nations while the gigantic crowds greet and cheer for them. Greece gets to go first, as they birthed the Olympics, and the rest of the nations enter in alphabetic order using the Greek alphabet. I like to imagine the hundreds of thousands of people gathered around their TV sets in the athletes' home countries to cheer them on as well. It takes a long time to watch all those athletes stream into the stadium, but it's still so moving to watch.

After more greetings and speeches, it's time for the entrance of the Olympic Torch, which has been traveling from Athens, Greece by special selected runners all these months. The crowd erupts in celebration as the final runner enters the stadium holding the golden torch and makes his or her way to a gigantic Olympic cauldron where the flame is finally lit. The Olympics have officially begun.

There is nothing else like the Olympic Opening Ceremonies. Can you think of anything else that brings our planet together in such a colorful, cultural celebration? These epic ceremonies give us goosebumps, I believe, because they point us to heaven. Here's a window into heaven from the book of Revelation:

The nations will walk by its light, and the kings of the earth will bring their splendor into it.... The glory and honor of the nations will be brought into it. (Revelation 21:24,26)

The kings of the earth marching in with their colorful, multi-national splendor. The glory and honor of all the nations, long parades of praise with every tribe, tongue and nation represented! All around are festive flags, traditional dances, lively symphonies and deeply rich cultural songs, a multi-national feast of the senses. (I personally can't wait to see the delegations from Southeast Asia come to the party.)

In his book, *Life Without Lack*, Dallas Willard uses the palette of Hebrews Chapter 11 to paint a welcoming picture of heaven. This passage contrasts the fearful Old Covenant experience Moses and the Israelites had at Mount Sinai with the joyful New Covenant welcome of Christ at Mount Zion. Willard wrote:

> That is the reality of heaven! It is where we stand, with God at the center, surrounded by all his perfect and perfected beings, those who have come to God through Jesus, the Lamb of God whose blood does not call out for judgment and condemnation, but for mercy, forgiveness, and the fullness of the grace of God! Indeed, it calls for a "festal gathering" (Heb. 12:22)—a grand, eternal, joyous party of praise to the God who makes it all possible![64]

Sounds fun to me! It will be more like an exciting global party than a septic waiting room where we wish we had brought a magazine. That "grand, joyous party of praise to God" is worth getting amped up for now.

Flawless Perfection

The first time I got to the end of C.S. Lewis' *Chronicles of Narnia* series, I remember tearing up when I got to this passage from *The Last Battle* (which I quoted earlier, but its brilliance is worth repeating):

It was the Unicorn who summed up what everyone was feeling. He stamped his right fore-foot on the ground and neighed, and then cried, "I have come home at last. This is my real country. I belong here. This is the land I have been looking for all my life, though I never knew it till now. The reason why we loved the old Narnia is that sometimes it looked a little like this."[65]

Something about that quote touched me profoundly. As I read it to my kids at bedtime, I remember playing the strong dad card and trying not to let them hear me choke up.

In Chapter Seven, I wrote about the longing for the *epipháne* of Christ and how He will reward that holy yearning with the Crown of Righteousness. Part of that *epipháne* longing is finally being free from disease, decay and destruction. Ageless, perfect, eternally healthy bodies exploring a perfectly beautiful place! Its decorator is the very same one who came up with the Great Barrier Reef, the Grand Canyon and the Amazon Rain Forest. The new heaven and the new earth are His grand finale masterpiece. Amazing is too weak a word to describe it...more like awestruck wonder for eternity.

To help us understand our deep ache for this feast-for-the-senses perfection a little more fully, let me bring back in the unicorn quote creator, C.S. Lewis. He writes about our unfulfilled longings on earth, how they show us that we were meant for "another world" and how they point us toward heaven:

Probably earthly pleasures were never meant to satisfy it, but only to arouse it, to suggest the real thing. If that is so, I must take care, on the one hand, never to despise, or to be unthankful for, these earthly blessings, and on the other, never to mistake them for the something else of which they are only a kind of copy, or echo, or mirage. I must keep alive in myself the desire for my true country, which I shall not find till after death; I must never let it get snowed under or turned aside; I must make it the main object of life to press on to that country and to help others to do the same.[66]

Lewis argues that every time beauty takes our breath away, it is a hint in our souls that exposes our longing for the perfection of heaven, the "true country." It's hard to put into words because this ache is so core to our souls:

We cannot tell it because it is a desire for something that has never actually appeared in our experience. We cannot hide it because our experience is constantly suggesting it, and we betray ourselves like lovers at the mention of a name. Our commonest expedient is to call it beauty and behave as if that had settled the matter...The books or the music in which we thought the beauty was located will betray us if we trust to them; it was not in them, it only came through them, and what came through them was longing.

These things—the beauty, the memory of our own past—are good images of what we really desire; but if they are mistaken for the thing itself, they turn into dumb idols, breaking the hearts of their worshippers. For they are not the thing itself; they are only the scent of a flower we have not found, the echo of a tune we have not heard, news from a country we have never yet visited.[67]

The next time a scene in nature moves you and somehow tinges you with a touch of sadness because it is so delicate and fleeting, believe what Lewis is telling us. You just got a sneak peek into the new creation of the "far-off country," and you won't be fully satisfied until you are finally there. And when you are finally there—hallelujah!—like Jewel, the unicorn of Narnia, you can say, "I have come home at last. This is my real country. I belong here. This is the land I have been looking for all my life."

Glorious Consummation

Another experience that gives me goosebumps is attending a wedding, and especially the part when a beautifully adorned bride walks gracefully down the aisle toward her beaming groom.

Just like the opening ceremonies of the Olympics, just like the beauty of nature both satisfies and stirs a deeper longing in our souls, a wedding ceremony is painting a picture for us of this longed-for moment of the groom and bride finally coming together in forever and unseparated love.

At my own wedding, one of our friends sang "How Beautiful," a popular worship song at the time by Twila Paris. This one line from that song still gives me goosebumps today for the same reason:

How beautiful the radiant Bride
who waits for her Groom
with His light in her eyes.[68]

The radiant bride walking toward the groom with the light of his love in her eyes. Imagine that anticipatory moment at a wedding between dear friends whom you know well. You feel a tender joy at this part in the ceremony because you are part of their story, and you are convinced they are so right for each other. Might be time for a tissue dab.

This is the ultimate deep calling to deep, the longing for union between the Christ and His beautifully adorned, unblemished Bride. Paul called this union a "profound mystery" (Ephesians 5:32), so it's no wonder that we need to dab tears away at weddings. Seeing the groom and bride finally come together in forever love and commitment is a little sneak preview of what is to come for us at the Marriage Supper of the Lamb:

> Then I heard what sounded like a great multitude, like the roar of rushing waters and like loud peals of thunder, shouting:
>
> "Hallelujah!
>   For our Lord God Almighty reigns.
> Let us rejoice and be glad
>   and give him glory!
>
> For the wedding of the Lamb has come,
>   and his bride has made herself ready.
> Fine linen, bright and clean,
>   was given her to wear." (Revelation 19:6-8)

Finally together and finally forever! We will no longer be marred by sin and scarred by shame. The Bride is fully restored and beautifully dressed in the righteousness of Christ. The epoch of unhindered union has begun.

Later in John's Revelation, we get one last peek at this wedding ceremony of the ages. The Bride is coming down out of heaven as the new Jerusalem, the place where God's Kingdom is finally and fully realized, "prepared as a bride, beautifully dressed for her husband" (Revelation 21:2).

That one scene may be enough to give you goosebumps for eternity. It certainly is meant to motivate us for a lifetime of purity and devotion to Christ on earth.

Staggering Honor

I have one last moved-me-to-tears confession to make, and this one is more embarrassing. I mean lots of people cry at weddings, but how many people tear up watching a reality TV show?

These admitted tears came on a 14-hour flight from Hong Kong to Los Angeles, when I was watching an episode of a reality TV show called "Undercover Boss."[69] Thankfully the plane was darkened so nobody saw my shame. (I hate it when my family catches me crying during movies or TV shows.)

You may have seen the show or know the concept. Jet-setting CEOs discard their fancy suits and disguise themselves in blue-collar working garb, mixing it up with employees in the trenches to get a feel for what is really happening in the companies they lead. At the end of the show, the CEO's true identity is revealed and the unsuspecting employees get rewarded for how they performed in the presence of their stealth boss. Great concept.

In this episode, the CEO and president of DirecTV, Mike White, pretends he is an out-of-work salesman named Tom Peters who is participating in a special company program where cameras will follow two job candidates around during their training phases in the large satellite-TV company. Mike, as Tom, gets trained by different technicians and service representatives, all of whom evaluate his performance as a trainee.

A service technician named Phil shows Tom the ropes and how important it is to go the extra mile with the customer. During a drive from a new customer's house back to the warehouse, Phil shares about his own escape from drug addiction and his efforts to serve troubled kids in a youth ministry he leads.

Tom is also coached by a customer service representative named Chloe who seems always to have a positive attitude with frustrated customers while troubleshooting with them on the phone. Over lunch she shares how her background of living in foster care inspired her to want to go into law or business to help kids from difficult backgrounds. She does her shifts at DirecTV to work her way through college.

The dramatic crescendo of the show comes at the end when Tom the trainee reveals that he is really Mike the CEO of their 23-billion-dollar company.

Mike praises a dumbfounded Phil for his excellent training and customer service and rewards him by offering to adopt some of his suggestions company-wide, and, even more touching for Phil, gives a personal check of $5,000 toward Phil's ministry which will enable his youth group to go on a mission trip.

During a follow-up interview, Phil quotes from Proverbs: "Do you see someone skilled in their work? They will serve before kings; they will not serve before officials of low rank" (Proverbs 22:29).

"From the character of how you carry yourself one day you'll sit among kings and here I am sitting among a CEO," he said. "I feel real good about being rewarded right now for hard work, and the real work that I did, it was recognized."

Mike also reveals his true identity to a shocked Chloe and raves about her positive spirit, even with difficult customers. He announces that DirecTV is starting a scholarship program for employees and that she will be the first recipient. He also offers to meet with her regularly to help mentor her in her promising career.

Through tears she asks, "Can I give you a hug?"

Something moved me in how these everyday people, struggling through their lives and trying to be decent human beings, were honored and rewarded by their boss.

The deeper reason why this "Undercover Boss" episode gave me misty eyes is that it strikes a deep chord in my soul, reminding me that God sees and ultimately rewards. You and I are living in a storyline in which the great author and perfecter of our faith is waiting at the finish line. He's got honor in mind for you at your life's grand-finale episode. He is like no boss you have ever had, thankfully. Our King is "gentle and humble in heart" (Matthew 11:29), and throughout your entire life He has been looking forward to bestowing you with heaven's honor and granting you a glorious reward.

If you could watch just a sneak peek of that final episode now, you would realize that one drop of heaven's honor is worth a whole lifetime of humble service and nameless obscurity on earth.

Our Undercover Boss is a Stealth King, humble and gentle in heart yet righteous and regal. He submitted to lowly servanthood during His sojourn on earth and ultimately even to humiliation, yet on that Day we will behold Him in His full, glorious kingship. We will be stunned when we fully realize that our acts of service on earth, when we thought no one was looking, were being filmed by heaven's secret cameras. What a shocker it will be to find out at the grand finale that our Stealth King was impersonating broken people all around us.

In the Parable of the Sheep and the Goats, Jesus said that we will be rewarded in whatever way we served the hungry, thirsty, homeless, unclothed, sick and imprisoned:

> The King will reply, "Truly I tell you, whatever you did for one of the least of these brothers and sisters of mine, you did for me." (Matthew 25:40)

Think about that for a minute. Every time we took the opportunity to care for the broken, we were really serving the true King of Kings. On the same day that the glory of our King is finally revealed, our glory will finally be revealed too.

I know, I know, that makes me squirm, too. (That's what Chapter Four was all about.) But keep in mind the biblical definition of glory, that sense of a full unveiling of something wonderful that makes you go, "Whoa!"

I love how C.S. Lewis defined it in *The Weight of Glory*:

For glory means good report with God, acceptance by God, response, acknowledgement, and welcome into the heart of things. The door on which we have been knocking all our lives will open at last.[70]

Welcome into the heart of things! On this glorious Day, at the Judgment Seat of Christ, we will be so awestruck, even in our new resurrection bodies. And the double jaw-dropper is that this resplendent King Jesus is smiling and has our reward in His hand.

Wait, is that a smile on His face? Is that for you? He seems to want you to know how much you mean to Him, how each little act of service deeply touched His heart. The door for acceptance and recognition on which you have been knocking all your life is opening at last! The glory you have been searching for all this while is fully and finally right in front of you, right in His hand.

Worth Imagining

Heaven is going to be so awesome it will make a multimillion-dollar Olympic ceremony extravaganza overseen by an Academy Award-winning director seem like a poorly acted high school drama in a school district that was facing budget cuts and couldn't afford any sets or costumes.

The scenery of heaven is so breathtaking, only those trained trekkers on earth who have climbed to the summit of Mount Everest under a canopy of a billion stars and then watched the sun slowly rise over the Himalayan mountain range the next morning, using the very best adjectives they could possibly think up, could barely begin to describe a backup drainage ditch there.

The Wedding Feast of the Lamb will make the next royal and regal wedding at Westminster Abbey look like a couple of drunk people getting hitched in a Las Vegas wedding chapel because they found a coupon in a complimentary casino magazine and decided to tie the knot spontaneously.

Next to the King of Kings, the Undercover Boss of television fame will seem like a tight-fisted miser passing out $5 gift cards as Christmas bonuses, while his underpaid employees try to feign smiles of appreciation.

Honor from and for the King

We've got heaven all wrong. In our fossilized thinking, it's a seemingly dull place that doesn't stir our imaginations and therefore doesn't impact our lives day-to-day. I want us to think of heaven rather as the celebratory and glorious place that it is, much like an athlete waking up early to train would imagine standing on the Olympic podium in a packed stadium and being presented with a gold medal.

Where my analogy breaks down, however, is that the Olympics only go as far as celebrating the glory of the athletes. That will for sure happen in heaven, and that's the main point I'm trying to make in this book—you and I will be honored there, like it or not. That understanding fuels a well-lived life, and at the finish line our glory will be fully revealed. But the greatest joy of heaven is that *His* glory will be fully revealed.

We have a small glimpse of this glory reveal party when the Apostle John encountered Jesus in heaven for the first time. This simple fisherman's life had been transformed by the traveling rabbi when he was a young man. John followed Jesus for three years of his life and had ample opportunities to behold the Messiah's power. With his own eyes he saw Jesus heal crippled people hundreds of times and even raise the dead on a few occasions. He witnessed Jesus bend the laws of physics toward His will by walking on water and making bread and fish appear right in His hands like magic. In the Last Supper story of his own Gospel, John identified himself as "the disciple whom Jesus loved" (John 13:23), right before Jesus revealed to him the identity of the betrayer. John was not only a disciple but a confidant, a BFF if you will. This "beloved disciple" (a moniker he used for himself six times) remained faithful to his Savior until he was an old man in exile on a prison island. Throughout his entire adult life, he walked with Jesus in a union of fellowship few of us could even imagine.

And here is what happened when John, so very familiar with Jesus as confidant and friend, finally beheld the Savior in His unhindered glory in that realm:

> I turned around to see the voice that was speaking to me. And when I turned I saw seven golden lampstands, and among the lampstands was someone like a son of man, dressed in a robe reaching down to his feet and with a golden sash around his chest. The hair on his head was white like wool, as white as snow, and his eyes were like blazing fire. His feet were like bronze glowing in a furnace, and his voice was like the sound of rushing waters. In his right hand he held seven stars, and coming out of his mouth was a sharp, double-edged sword. His face was like the sun shining in all its brilliance.

When I saw him, I fell at his feet as though dead. Then he placed his right hand on me and said: "Do not be afraid. I am the First and the Last. I am the Living One; I was dead, and now look, I am alive for ever and ever! And I hold the keys of death and Hades." (Revelation 1:12-18)

John really thought he knew who Jesus was through all his up-close-and-personal experience with Him, and then it's like he gets handed a pair of 3D glasses in heaven. In that moment he finally saw Jesus for who He really was, the glorious Son of Man popping out of the screen of John's limited experience of Him so far. John drops at His feet like a dead man. It was literally too much to handle, the ultimate experience of the weight of glory.

You and I have barely begun the journey of knowing Jesus. We have tasted and we have seen that the Lord is good, for sure, but when we get to heaven we will realize we had only tasted the smallest of appetizers before. Like John, we will find that our familiarity with Him was only the faintest hint of a beginning.

We've been seeing through a glass darkly and dimly, to use one of Paul's metaphors. Mirrors in those days were not refined and polished like ours today, but more like warped pieces of glass that offered back a distorted view. With that in mind, Paul said of that Day:

For now we see only a reflection as in a mirror; then we shall see face to face. Now I know in part; then I shall know fully, even as I am fully known. (1 Corinthians 13:12)

We will realize that the little bit of finite understanding we had of Jesus in our finite life was like looking at Him through a dark, warped piece of glass. Our understanding has been dim and dull our whole lives but on That Day it will be oh so bright. He will be fully seen and known at last. The illumination of God's glory in heaven is so intense, in fact, that it will light up heaven forever.

> The city does not need the sun or the moon to shine on it, for the glory of God gives it light, and the Lamb is its lamp. (Revelation 21:23)

No more dim understanding. God's glory bathing everything in brilliant illumination.

In heaven you'll receive your own pair of 3D glasses. Fitted with your new resurrection body, you'll be able to finally behold the awesome glory of the King of Kings. You'll be so glad in that moment that back during your time on earth, at some point on its fleeting timeline, you had decided to fully give your life to Him. It's so clear now. The best decision you ever made was to live toward His smile.

The Morning Star of the Show

In Revelation Chapter Four, a scene opens up for us in heaven of the four living creatures crying out their eternal song, "Holy, holy, holy is the Lord God Almighty, who was, and is, and is to come" (Revelation 4:8). Then we see twenty-four elders falling down, laying down their glorious crowns at His feet, and adding a new verse to this eternal worship:

You are worthy, our Lord and God,
to receive glory and honor and power,
for you created all things,
and by your will they were created
and have their being. (Revelation 4:11)

That is beautiful holiness for sure, but in the next chapter the glory is heightened and a little tension is added. All of heaven is looking for someone worthy to open the ancient scroll in the hand of God. No one can be found, which causes weeping. Then one of the twenty-four elders steps forward and says to John,

Do not weep! See, the Lion of the tribe of Judah, the Root of David, has triumphed. He is able to open the scroll and its seven seals. (Revelation 5:5)

When John turns to look, he doesn't see what he expects— the Lion of the tribe of Judah—but rather a Lamb, "looking as if it had been slain" (Revelation 5:6). After the introduction of this spotless and sacrificial Lamb, there is an eternal burst of adoration in heaven for this Uncreated One who was born to a simple village girl and placed in an animal's feeding trough. Praise is sustained for the Glorious One who was raised by a poor family and walked the dusty streets of earth, restored the broken, healed the sick, preached the truth and eventually surrendered Himself to violent men. His death on a crude cross was horrifying and made all of heaven shudder.

And now this perfect Lamb takes the scroll from the right hand of God, and then an even deeper, more profound worship erupts in a new song, accompanied by harps and a golden bowl full of incense:

> You are worthy to take the scroll and to open its seals,
> because you were slain, and with your blood
> you purchased for God persons
> from every tribe and language and people and nation.
> You have made them to be a kingdom
> and priests to serve our God,
> and they will reign on the earth. (Revelation 5:9-10)

Let's now put yourself there, where you will be one day and all days. The living creatures here are bizarre yet beautiful, and the unfathomably majestic angels take your breath away, but they did not walk through what the humble man from Galilee suffered through. They did not voluntarily walk to their own death, all because of God's love for people of every nation. They are worthy of your awe, but He is worthy of your adoration.

You join in the song with the countless thousands of angels encircling the throne, along with the elders and the living creatures, and all of you worship together:

> Worthy is the Lamb, who was slain,
> to receive power and wealth and wisdom and strength
> and honor and glory and praise! (Revelation 5:12)

Another layer of worship is added, this time by "every creature in heaven and on earth and under the earth and on the sea, and all that is in them" (Revelation 5:13). They cry out:

To him who sits on the throne and to the Lamb
be praise and honor and glory and power,
for ever and ever! (Revelation 5:13)

The four living creatures, who began the worship festival, add their heavenly exclamation point:

The four living creatures said, "Amen," and the elders
fell down and worshiped. (Revelation 5:14)

This here—this is a moment you could live in forever. You are grateful just to be here, to have gotten into this perfect place by His precious blood and to have a non-tiring body that can handle all the glorious awe that permeates from His Throne. You are thinking no other thought but to worship this Lamb Who Was Slain forever and ever, content to blend anonymously into this crowd of multitudes whose whole focus is on Him.

Your Turn

And then something surprising happens, something that jolts you out of your exuberant and satisfying worship. You don't know how long you have been worshipping because it would be impossible even to measure time in this realm. But somewhere along the way, at some point in this never-ending Day, you hear Him calling your name.

Your name? Why would any other name be uttered in this place besides that of the King of Kings and Lord of Lords?

Yes, you definitely hear Him uttering you name, and you dare not deflect or deny a summoning from the mouth of the resplendent King of Heaven. You step forward in heaven's courts, a place that pulsates with the perfection of holy intensity.

As you walk toward Him, your fully renewed heart is aflutter with anticipation and also nervousness, remembering all the struggles and failings of your life. You're lamenting the millions of shortcuts and compromises you took, and how your life was so much more about you than Him.

You can't bear to look up and behold His gaze, and instead you cast your ashamed eyes down at His feet, which are burnished like bronze glowing in a furnace. There on His feet, you can make out a nail-sized scar and you remember...the CROSS! Oh thank God, literally. His blood has covered all of your sin and shame, and He is summoning you here not for punishment but for reward!

Great relief washes over you. His amazing grace, which you sort of understood and could have defined theologically on earth, you are now experiencing extravagantly. It gives you the courage to dare to look up into His radiant face.

Oh that face! Eyes burning with fire that can peer into all creation, leaving everything uncovered and laid bare. You dare to look deeper into those eyes as He beckons you, knowing that it is by His grace that you can even stand before Him. In His direct gaze you behold a look of love which fills you with the most wonderful feeling you have ever experienced. You see joy through a bright smile beaming on His precious face!

Oh that smile! It's been the core longing of your heart all along, to know that even amid all your struggles and stumbles, you have somehow pleased the King of Kings with the meager sacrifice of your fleeting life.

You are standing before Him now, and His smile continues to bathe you in radiant light. You knew in the deepest parts of your soul that this moment was coming and now it's here, more glorious than you ever could have imagined with a thousand lifetimes on earth. Standing in front of the King of Kings with His full attention on you is almost too much to bear, even here.

He opens His mouth, and in a voice that sounds like many rushing waters, issues His verdict over your life.

Well done, good and faithful servant. Enter into the joy of your Master.

His smile is the most wonderful thing you have ever seen, and now it is matched with the most wonderful thing you have ever heard. With that one phrase, you are almost undone. Yet again you are thankful for your new resurrection body that enables you to stand before Him in His presence, as you would rather melt away in a puddle of tears through all eternity, just knowing that your life has somehow pleased this Glorious One.

You sense that even more is coming, that this radiant King is wanting to grant you even more. That smile and that phrase would have satisfied you through all eternity, but you dare not reject anything He would bestow. A thousand scriptures stream through your fully renewed mind and one comes to the surface: "Look, I am coming soon! My reward is with me, and I will give to each person according to what they have done" (Revelation 22:12). This promise, one that you didn't really think much on before, affirms your intuition and readies you. There is more honor on His mind.

His smile continues to radiate, and then, in front of all the resplendent angels and heavenly creatures, He bestows a very personal honor upon you, fitting you with a crown fashioned in heaven just for you. It's more magnificent than the most precious treasure you could have ever imagined on earth, and not just because of its ornateness, which is exquisite beyond measure. The reward represents His pleasure in you. In the bestowing, He tells how much He appreciated, in detail, the sacrifices and service of your life.

There is such intimate detail in what He reveals to you, instances of impact and names of people that you had forgotten. Some are even here and you can see them in your new periphery-heightened vision, all of them celebrating in exultation. As He continues, you are shocked to discover that even little acts of service that you thought almost nothing about moved His heart deeply. He opens your mind to remember all the times you cared for the drifting and the broken and it was really Him, every Gospel seed you sowed, and every specific instance of love shown for others motivated by His great love.

You realize fully that every word out of His mouth is refined gold so you dare not deflect the honor. This gloriously omniscient God could never say anything duplicitous or even slightly overexaggerated. You bow your head in humble acceptance, receiving His honor.

And your next thought, one that runs through the rest of eternity and still somehow doesn't seem long enough, is to cast that glorious crown right back at the feet of the Worthy One, worshiping and enjoying Him forever.

ACKNOWLEDGMENTS

Writing a book can be a bit of a lonely process, with lots of time in the cave by yourself. That's sometimes a challenge for an extrovert like me, so I am very grateful for the following people who not only gave me great edits and insights, but also lent to me the encouragement of their presence. The fellowship of their friendship was a warm light in my cave.

Thanks so much Bill Korver, Steve Hawthorne, John McComb, Jack Hammans, Jeff Fish, Mick Murray, Drew Steadman, Eric Bryant and Ron Parrish for your manuscript advice and dialogue around theology. I feel so enriched by your wisdom.

To Rob Stennett, Ben Taylor and Peter Nevland—your friendship is a treasure in my life. Thanks for conversations around framing the content to make it more engaging.

To Dan Campbell, Meredith Proffitt, Cat Wise, James Wise, Sarah Guerrero, Jim Baton, Michael Hayes, Steve Richart, Nicole Hollon, Kianna Greene, Taylor Mitchell, Deb Ploskonka and Susan Sills —I'm so honored that you took time to read over my manuscript and have so appreciated your excellent editorial feedback. Thanks also, Joel McDowell, for your formatting and technical assistance, and Marla Lackey, for your author advice.

To my family and especially my beautiful and gracious wife Stephanie who has been patient with me as I've slipped down another rabbit hole for this writing project. Wise King Solomon said, "A wife of noble character is her husband's crown" (Proverbs 12:4). You, amazing lady, are one dazzling crown.

ABOUT THE AUTHOR

Mike O'Quin Jr. served as a social entrepreneur in Indonesia for 14 years with his family. He currently lives in Southeast Asia where he serves in a pastoral role for an international missions organization.

Mike is married to his high school sweetheart Stephanie and together they have four kids, three grown and out of the house and one younger one still tagging along. He can still make all of their eyes roll with his corny dad jokes.

You can find Mike on Instagram @mikeoquin, Twitter @mikeoquin, and follow him on his blog at www.mikeoquin.com.

OTHER BOOKS BY MIKE O'QUIN JR.

Java Wake

Stephen Cranton's mid-life crisis is coming on a decade too early. On a business trip to Indonesia, he evaluates his heartless existence after getting challenged by an obnoxious adventure guide on his flight. Soon after landing, Stephen tries to spice up his stale life with a brazen act of spontaneity. Bad move. His impulsiveness sets off a chain of events, one that brings enemies into his life and endangers new friends. His longsuffering wife, who makes a spontaneous move of her own by flying to Java for a last-ditch marriage intervention, also gets tangled up in his miscalculation. Stephen feels like he is living inside a nightmare that he can't seem to escape, but will the ordeal be enough to wake up his sleeping heart?

"An atmospheric debut."

— *Kirkus Reviews*

Growing Desperate: The Favor of God for the Poor in Spirit

Desperate people stop Jesus in His tracks. Think of the woman hemorrhaging for 12 long years, despondent that all remedies up to that point had proven worthless. The only option left for her was to grab the robe of the miracle man as He walked by. Jesus affirmed her courage, healed her, called her daughter and blessed her in peace. Jesus admires your gut-honest desperation more than your religious self-sufficiency. It attracts Him like nothing else. Cruel circumstances, fractured relationships, bruised emotions and aching loneliness— God meets us in the desperate places of our lives, fights and delights to restore us, and sends us out into a world full of desperate people.

"Honesty is what you will find as you advance through the treasures that await you in this unforgettable book. The words are not the hollow ramblings of an academic, but rather the wisdom of a man who writes from the depths of his quest to find meaning and hope in the darkest and loneliest circumstances...I invite you to read his meditations on human desperation. Prepare your heart. I dare say, you will never be the same."

— Paul Richardson, author of *A Certain Risk: Living Your Faith at the Edge* (Zondervan, 2010)

RECOMMENDED RESOURCES FOR FURTHER STUDY

All Things New, John Eldredge (HarperCollins Publishers, 2017)

Biblical Use of Rewards as a Motivation for Christian Service, Dr. Bill F. Korver (Dissertation at Liberty University, 2011)

Facing Your Final Job Review, Woodrow Kroll (Crossway, 2008)

Final Destiny, Joseph C. Dillow (Grace Theology Press, 2018)

Heaven, Randy Alcorn (Tyndale Momentum, 2004)

Imagine Heaven, John Burke (Baker Books, 2015)

The Journey of Desire, John Eldredge (Thomas Nelson, 2016)

The Judgment Seat of Christ, D.M. Panton (Schoettle Publishing Company, 1984)

The Judgment Seat of Christ, Rick Howard (Naioth Sound and Publishing, 1980)

The Law of Rewards, Randy Alcorn (Tyndale Momentum, 2003)

Life Without Lack, Dallas Willard (Nelson Books, 2018)

Suffering, Martyrdom, and Rewards in Heaven, Josef Ton (The Romanian Missionary Society, 2000)

Surprised By Hope, N. T. Wright (HarperCollins Publishers, 2008)

This Was Your Life!, Rick Howard and Jamie Lash (Chosen Books, 1998)

The Weight of Glory, C.S. Lewis (HarperCollins Publishers, 1980)

Your Eternal Reward, Erwin W. Lutzer (Moody Publishers, 2005)

ENDNOTES

1 Marin Luther, "This Day and That Day" (Lewis Guest IV, 2020) desiringgod.org/articles/this-day-and-that-day.

2 Charles Spurgeon, *A Discourse Upon True Blessedness Here and Hereafter*, ccel.org/ccel/spurgeon/sermons31/sermons31.lix.html.

3 Jim Elliot, *The Journals of Jim Elliot*, October 28, 1949 entry, Billy Graham Center of Wheaton College, last modified January 2016.

4 C.S. Lewis, *The Weight of Glory* (New York: HarperCollins Publishers, 1980), 26.

5 C.S. Lewis, *Mere Christianity* (New York: HarperCollins Publishers, 1980), 134.

6 J.I. Packer, *Knowing God* (Downers Grove, IL: InterVarsity Press, 1993), 169.

7 Josef Tson, *Suffering, Martyrdom, and Rewards in Heaven* (Wheaton, IL: The Romanian Missionary Society, Reprinted 2000), 416.

8 Patrick Lencioni, *The Motive* (Hoboken, New Jersey: John Wiley & Sons, 2020).

9 C.S. Lewis, *The Weight of Glory* (New York: HarperCollins Publishers, 1980).

10 *Minta Tolong!* Asia Media Productions, RCTI, GTV (Indonesia).

11 C.S. Lewis, *The Weight of Glory* (New York: HarperCollins Publishers, 1980), 26.

12 Martin Luther, as translated by Herbert Bouman, *The Doctrine of Justification in the Lutheran Confessions*, Concordia Theological Monthly 26 (November 1955), No. 11.

13 D.M. Panton, *The Judgment Seat of Christ* (Havesville, NC: Schoettle Publishing Company, 1984), 3.

[14] Dr. Bill F. Korver, *Biblical Use of Rewards as a Motivation for Christian Service*, Dissertation at Liberty University (2011), 38.

[15] Christian Smith and Melinda Denton, *Soul Searching: The Religious and Spiritual Lives of American Teenagers* (New York: Oxford University Press, 2005).

[16] N.T. Wright, *Surprised by Hope* (New York: HarperCollins, 2008).

[17] C.S. Lewis, *The Lion, the Witch, and the Wardrobe* (New York: HarperCollins Publishers, 1978), 79-80.

[18] Leonard Ravenhill, *The Judgement Seat of Christ* (Lindale, Texas: 1994), ravenhill.org.

[19] Helen Thomas (Executive Producer) and Tom Coveney (Series Producer), *Astronauts: Do You Have What It Takes?* BBC Studios, U.S. Re-Title: *Astronauts: Toughest Job in the Universe*, 2017.

[20] Ibid

[21] C.H. Spurgeon, "The Judgment Seat of God" sermon, printed in *Metropolitan Tabernacle Pulpit* (Volume 27, 1881).

[22] Appian, *Roman History,* series of monographs printed in Venice 1477 by Erhard Ratdolt, Chisholm, Hugh, ed., "Appian," *Encyclopædia Britannica.* 2 (Cambridge University Press, 1911) pp. 221-222.

[23] agathos - Strong's Greek Lexicon #18 (KJV), Blue Letter Bible, Outline of Biblical Usage.

[24] Woodroll Kroll, *Facing Your Final Job Review* (Chicago, IL: Crossway, 2008), 78.

[25] Nida, Eugene A., and Charles R. Taber, *The Theory and Practice of Translation, With Special Reference to Bible Translating,* (Leiden: Brill, 1969).

[26] Courtney Handman, *Critical Christianity: Translation and Denominational Conflict in Papua New Guinea* (Oakland, CA: University of California Press, 2015), 84.

[27] Hugh Hudson (Director), *Chariots of Fire* (1981) Allied Stars; Goldcrest Films.

[28] Langdon Gilkey, *Shantung Compound* (New York: Harper & Row, 1966).

[29] Eric Liddell, commonly attributed quote upon his return to Scotland after the 1924 Summer Olympics, "Eric Liddell" christianity.org.uk/article/eric-liddell.

[30] Steven C. Hawthorne, "The Story of His Glory," *Perspectives on the World Christian Movement* (Pasadena, William Carey Publishing, 2009), 50.

[31] Steven C. Hawthorne, "The Honor and Glory of Jesus Christ: Heart of the Gospel and the Mission of God," *Honor, Shame and the Gospel* (Pasadena, William Carey Publishing, 2020), 4.

[32] George Bennard (Composer), Hymn, "The Old Rugged Cross" (1912) Refrain.

[33] poimainō - Strong's Greek Lexicon #4165 (KJV), Blue Letter Bible, Outline of Biblical Usage.

[34] Corrie ten Boom, *The Hiding Place* (New York, Bantam Books, 1984).

[35] Ibid

[36] Ibid

[37] Polycarp, commonly attributed quote, Dan Graves, "Article 7" (Christian History Institute) christianhistoryinstitute.org/incontext/article/polycarp-testimony.

[38] Polycarp, commonly attributed quote, Joseph Hattrop, "Faithful In The Fire: The Christian Legacy Of St Polycarp" (2017) christiantoday.com/article/faithful.in.the.fire.the.christian.legacy.of.saint.polycarp/104969.htm.

[39] R.W. Cargill, St. Monans, *A Goodly Heritage* (John Ritchie, 2017) believersmagazine.com/bm.php?i=20130703.

[40] *Biography of Dietrich Bonhoeffer*, The Dietrich Bonhoeffer Institute, tdbi.org/dietrich-bonhoeffer/biography/.

[41] Ibid

[42] Eric Metaxas, *Bonhoeffer: Pastor, Martyr, Prophet, Spy* (Nashville, TN: Nelson Books, 2020).

[43] Matthew Henry Bible Commentary, James 1 (Verses 2-12, section IV) christianity.com.commentary.

[44] Dr. Arthur Freeman "Gemeine: Count Nikolaus von Zinzendorf's Understanding of the Church," *The Durnbaugh Lecture*, March 25, 1999, Young Center for the Study of Anabaptist and Pietist Groups (Elizabethtown, PA: Brethren Life and Thought, 2002).

[45] John Wesley (Composer), Hymn, "I Thirst, Thou Wounded Lamb of God" (1740).

[46] John Burke, *Imagine Heaven* (Grand Rapids, MI: Baker Books, 2015), 55.

[47] C.S. Lewis, *Mere Christianity* (New York: HarperCollins Publishers, 1980), 136-137.

[48] Warren Wiersbe, *The Bible Exposition Commentary, Pentateuch* (Colorado Springs, CO: Victor, 2001), 255.

[49] C.T. Studd, as quoted in eaec.org/faithhallfame/ctstudd.htm.

[50] Sally McClung, Prayer for Sally and Floyd McClung Update, *Facebook*, July 7, 2020, 12:27 p.m., facebook.com/floydmcclungprayer/posts/1685285944943201.

[51] Marcus Warner and Jim Wilder, *Rare Leadership: 4 Uncommon Habits For Increasing Trust, Joy, and Engagement in the People You Lead* (Chicago: Moody Publishers, 2016), Kindle Edition, 204.

[52] Dallas Willard, *Life Without Lack* (Nashville, TN: Nelson Books, 2018), 20.

[53] E.E. Hewitt (Composer), Hymn, "When We All Get to Heaven," 1898.

[54] Miriam Rockness, Blog Post, "Reflections on the Art and Writings of Lilias Trotter," *About Lilias*, March 5 2012, ililiastrotter.wordpress.com/about/.

[55] Lilias Trotter, *Parables of the Cross*, (London; Edinburgh: Marshall Brothers, 1890) 63-64.

[56] Gary Larson, "Wish I'd Brought a Magazine" (Cartoon), *The Far Side*, (Kansas City, MO: Universal Press Syndicate, 1985).

[57] John Eldredge, *The Journey of Desire* (New York: Thomas Nelson, 2016).

[58] Wright, N. T., *Surprised by Hope* (New York: HarperOne, 2008).

[59] Ibid

[60] Dallas Willard, *The Divine Conspiracy* (New York: HarperOne, 1997)

[61] John Eldredge and Craig McConnell, *Wild at Heart Podcast* (2008) wildatheart.org/podcast

[62] Richard Foster, *Celebration of Discipline: The Path to Spiritual Growth* (New York: HarperCollins Publishers, 1998), 25-26.

[63] John Burke, *Imagine Heaven* (Grand Rapids, MI: Baker Books, 2015), 105.

[64] Dallas Willard, Life Without Lack (Nashville, TN: Nelson Books, 2018), 41.

[65] C.S. Lewis, *The Last Battle* (New York: HarperCollins Publishers, 1984), 196.

[66] C.S. Lewis, *Mere Christianity* (New York: HarperCollins Publishers, 1980), 120-121.

[67] C.S. Lewis, *The Weight of Glory* (New York: HarperCollins Publishers, 1980), 30-31.

[68] Twila Paris (Artist), "How Beautiful" (1990).

[69] *Undercover Boss*, DirecTV, episode 3, Studio Lambert, October 10, 2010.

[70] C.S. Lewis, *The Weight of Glory* (New York: HarperCollins Publishers, 1980), 30-31.